More Praise for

The New Revised
Catechlysm

"A brave new source for authoritative doctrinal piffle."
—Roman Collier, author, *The 30-Minute Priest*

"We can practically hear the limits of the First Amendment creaking. It's right up there with parking lot tailgate parties as a celebration of tasteless freedom."
—A Saint Louis Cardinal

"Takes a whack at the sacred cow piñata of the Church and gives up lots of surprisingly satisfying bull in the process!" —*Self Mortification for Dummies*

"Stands like a Colossus, astride the tawdry little world of cheap parody." —Liberation Theology Cruise Lines

The New Revised
Catechlysm

Edited by
Brother Paul, D.U.I.

Uenial Press

ISBN: 978-0-9847941-0-2

Bless us with your virtual presence at: Catechlysm.com

Project Editor: Michael Wilt, TuckerSeven.com
Cover Design: Brad Norr, BradNorrDesign.com
Illustrations: Cleofe Pacaña

About the Author

After a lifetime of the most strenuous Catholicism, Brother Paul, D.U.I. is now happily settled, living in pre-absolved sin with his partner, Rebecca, on their sprawling 0.11-acre ranchette, "Amazing Graze." He spends his days raising prize-winning heirloom guilt and herds of Protestant carpenter ants, which seem determined to eat the life-sized cross near his mailbox, as well as the increasingly wooden features of his own aged face. In the evenings, according to the strict rule of Saint Pinot Noir, he enjoys a chalice of something strong.

IMPRIMI POTEST:	Ludicristo Confabulo, D.M.V., D.O.A.
	Vaticanus Cryptogrammaticus
NIHIL OBSTAT:	Neil Obstat, O.M.G., K.F.C.
	Censer Cannibisus
IMPRIMATUR:	$Most Rev. Consonantimus
	Wzgyckwcz
	Cardinal Archbishop of Dubai

For Alan and Helen
"What we all so dearly want is for someone to tell us
what to do."

And for Rebecca,
the one in a billion geek

Men never do evil so completely and cheerfully as when they do it from religious conviction.

—Blaise Pascal

A man was walking alone on a forest path, with Satan and his favorite demon following at a distance. The man stopped, bent over, and picked up something. The demon, horrified, exclaimed, "Oh no, Master! The man has discovered Truth!" Satan smiled and said, "Oh, don't worry about that. I'm going to help him organize it."

—as recounted by
J. Krishnamurti

CONTENTS

Part III: The Sacraments and Prayer 103

ACKNOWLEDGEMENTS

Thanks go out to the following Congregations who took time to read daft copies of The New Revised Catechlysm, offering many hilarious suggestions, all of which were taken very seriously before being discarded. After all, the true author of this book is Christ, and will He ever be pissed if He finds out someone has stuck a huge siphon hose in His royalty account:

The Sisters of Temerity
The Asbestos Sisters of the Divine Fire
The Brothers of Gradual Weight-Loss
The Society of Jargon
Oblate Brothers of the Bolo Tie
The Discalced Rule Followers of Dominic When
    He Was Still a Nice Guy
The Blogostinian Fathers
The Order of the Borderline Have-Nots
The Sisters of Extreme Fundraising
The Confraternity of Charitable Infighting
The Mission Fathers of Hellish Introspection
The Chlamydian Order
The Cloistered Sisters of the Sacred Mini-Bar

NOTE FOR THE TEACHER'S EDITION

The New Revised Catechlysm is designed to prevent confusion in the students. There are questions, there are answers. Period. The little gnomes need to learn right off that it is all about memorizing. Long experience has taught us that the twin inspirations of the power of the Holy Spirit and an appropriate whupping will bring them to the Truth with a minimum of bedwetting. It may not seem entirely natural to instruct ten-year-olds on how to pray for a happy death, or on the best ways to perform the Last Rites (or Xtreme Unction, as we are now calling it), but when you witness the powerful personality changes that these and other lessons engender in the students, you will feel nothing but gratification.

You must be vigilant about the students' sly efforts to subtly change the answers—substituting an indefinite for a definite article, for example. They are bound by the laws of their sinful natures to try subverting the memorization of God's rules, so you must be stern in the loving wallopings you provide for them, patiently explaining that in Hell they will get no "over-sies", no do-overs, no mulligans. And remember: every hour you have not occupied them with this rote memorization is an hour they are likely to be spending pushing or pulling on their private parts.

Do not hesitate to use the Exercises included in each chapter, but do not roll them up and strike the students with them, or at least not about the face and head. When unrolled, these provide a thorough review and adaptation of the lesson just completed by the pupil, giving him some reason to suspect that the issues addressed might actually have modest application in the world.

TO THE STUDENT

Boys and girls, the point of this book is for you to have fun with God. When Christ said, "Suffer the little children to come unto me," He was under the influence of an antiquated translation, and would never mean to cause suffering to you or anyone else. Well, okay, there were those money changers He threw out of the temple. And all the people in Hell. Maybe anyone who would toss a sloppy, gratuitous pedophile joke into this paragraph. But that's it. The truth is that Jesus of course longs to have you near Him, but has just enough time for a couple of groups of eight to ten kids—a hug, taking a couple of pictures, maybe curing a stutter. Everyone understands that the Lord has a bruising schedule.

At the same time, you should understand that The New Revised Catechlysm is not leaving everything up to you. It is not one of those deals where we throw a lot of stuff at the wall and see what sticks. What are you: ten, eleven, maybe twelve years old? You're not even old enough to know which religious order you want to join. So the Catechlysm is here to see that you accept even the bits of doctrine that seem like the crudest twaddle, since all of it is necessary to mold you into the kind of courageous people who can face fear and guilt and make a lifestyle out of them.

All of this through the executive arm of that Holy Mother of a Church that somehow got married to God, and of which union you are the happy issue.

Brother Paul, D.U.I
Napa, California

PRAYERS FOR EVERY DAY

This section should include such all-time, solid gold barn-burners as the Sign of the Cross, the Lord's Prayer, the Hail Mary, and the Acts of Faith, Hope, Charity, Abstention, Lassitude, and Recklessness. These are all valuable prayers, no doubt about it. But when you think *prayer*, you must also think *indulgences*. These are the currency you can amass from the practice of prayer, as you would from collecting cereal box tops to get a personal cordless vibrator. But this currency, once acquired, will allow you to buy some time off of your sentence in Purgatory when you die. It's like money in the bank!

So you need to know how to acquire your "fortune" in the most effective and efficient possible way. And the way to do that is: Ejaculations.

You wish. That's *not* what we mean. Clean up your thoughts—NOW.

An ejaculation is a short, fervent prayer (cut it *out*!) that is easily among the highest-yielding of all. For example, you could drone on for a full thirty seconds reciting a beautiful prayer like the "Hail, Holy Queen", which will net you five years less in Purgatory. Not bad for a half-minute's work. But now, check out one of the powerhouse ejaculations (we *won't* warn you again). You can spend less than five seconds saying, "Most Sacred Heart of Jesus, have mercy on us" and walk away with a 500-day indulgence. Do the math. In that same thirty seconds you can net ten to twelve years less in Purgatory! The smart money will always go for an ejaculation.

PART I

THE APOSTLES' CREED

LESSON 1

THE PURPOSE OF MAN'S EXISTENCE

To Help Get You Through This Lesson

God is the Supreme Being who has always existed, even before Dick Clark's Rockin' New Year's Eve. He made everything. All of us are appreciative of that, even though there have been numerous reports of Him not honoring His warranties. Not a man or a woman, a tree or a bird, or anything else could keep on existing unless God wills it, which is a powerful truth that unfortunately makes it pretty hard to relax around Him.

He especially made you to show forth His goodness, and, even if you think he botched your nose or could have given you a bigger winkie, He still intends to share with you His everlasting happiness in Heaven.

You might ask: So why aren't we there right now? Why don't we just follow the Pearly Brick Road, or whatever?

Well, it's not quite that simple. As the U.S. Deputy Secretary for Spiritual Affairs recently testified before the Senate Permanent Subcommittee on Metaphysics and Bible History, "Regarding humankind's very early history, as many of you know: Mistakes were made." And because of those mistakes, we now have to do certain things to "gain" Heaven, like contestants on a meta-reality show.

Sort of like "Survivor" meets "The Great Race," but with Jesus Christ providing the directions. Trust us on this: You do *not* want to get voted off the island.

This first lesson, and the entire New Revised Cate-chlysm, is really about plotting a course to that everlasting happiness, but doing it without seeming too desperate or cold-blooded. That's the key. It is through the example of Jesus Christ, God's son and mouthpiece, that you can learn exactly how to be truly happy—and with the right motivation, too! Stay with us on this fantastic journey, and you'll end up so clean and pure that everyone will re-mark on your wonderful "new car" smell.

Who is God?
God is the Supreme Being, so perfect in all things that, candidly, it gets a little annoying. He made all things and keeps them in existence, generally keeping His regrets to Himself and lashing out only rarely.

Why did God make us?
A question He certainly must often ask Himself.

What must we do to gain the happiness of Heaven?
To gain the happiness of Heaven, we must know, love, serve, and suck up to God in this world. Just remember, it's way worth having a brown nose for awhile if in the end you can collect on the heavenly reward. As the proverb goes, he who laughs last probably lied about a lot of stuff or fudged the numbers.

From whom do we learn to know, love, serve, and suck up to God?
Depending on whom you talk to, there is a wide range of answers, from Paul Krugman to Dorothy Parker to Davy

Crockett. There is a perennial strong show of support for both Richelieu and Paul McCartney. Finally, though, the go-to person for this kind of learning is Jesus Christ, who as the Son of God obviously has the inside track as well as having His Catholic Church, a rock-solid engine for cross-platform market penetration, with its thousands of branch offices around the world.

Where do we find the chief truths taught by Jesus Christ through the Catholic Church?

Wherever you go to find them, it should be a bonafide source. The subject matter is serious enough that you don't want to get caught just pulling them out of your butt. You can always Google the chief truths. Or maybe try Wikipedia, we hear they're pretty strong. If you don't want to go online, you can always find the chief truths taught by Jesus Christ in the Apostles' Creed.

What is the Apostles' Creed?

The Apostles' Creed is like a combination of a prayer, a loyalty oath, and a Double Dog Dare. It's a list of items you *must* believe if you want to be Catholic, so the authorities have made some of them deliberately UNbelievable just to make sure not just anyone gets through the turnstile. Believing some of these items is like taking the dare of your friends to steal the magazine, eat the worms, or drop your pants in the middle of the little league field.

Say the Apostles' Creed. (To save you time and effort, we will ask only that you say the "Speed Creed" (or Credo Speedo) instituted by Pope Dexedrinius IV just before his tragic death from placebo overdose in A.D. 1268.)

I Believe in God, in Jesus Christ who was conceived, born, suffered, crucified, died, buried, descended, arose, ascended, sits, and will judge. I believe in the Holy Ghost, as much as in the final five items, which I take as read. Amen.

Exercises

1) God is the Supreme Being who made all things and keeps them: (a) on edge; (b) heavily sedated; (c) in the dark; (d) squabbling among themselves.

2) List and explain all the reasons God made us. Be sure to include our strong re-sale value, and the amazing number of tax deductions He gets each year.

3) Discuss: If a girl loves her radio more than her rosary beads, is she going full speed toward Heaven? As part of your answer, detail the optimum speed for travel toward Heaven (without being reckless), and whether this girl has deep psychological issues stemming from this competitive fixation between her radio and her rosary. Does poor reception on the rosary beads account for her preferring the radio?

LESSON 2

GOD AND HIS PERFECTIONS

"I believe in God, the Father Almighty,
who sure plays a mean pinball . . ."

To Help Get You Through This Lesson

Spirits are the highest form of beings in all existence. Because they have no bodies, they do not need toilet paper, beer coasters, a monthly bikini wax, or friends. God is the greatest of these spirits because he is *self-existing* (like the best oven is self-cleaning), unlike the Ghost of Christmas Past, Casper, and the Spirit of Saint Louis, all of which rely heavily on receipts from licensing contracts.

His perfections (good qualities) are infinite, which is why we say God is *infinitely perfect*, and why He can be such a bore after He's had a few drinks at a party. By contrast, the perfections of His creatures are finite—though sometimes you'll swear some of them have *in*finite *im*perfections if you're around them long enough.

Just by using our mind, or *natural reason*, we can know that the world could have been made only by an infinite God. Since, however, few Catholics ever use their natural reason, God also reveals much information about Himself through *supernatural revelation* from three sources: (1) Sacred Scripture (the Bible and Hunter S. Thompson's books); (2) Tradition (holy teachings like the

Catechlysm); and (3) a great website called *Begoodand-shutup.hvn.*

What is a spirit?
A spirit is a being that has understanding, free will, and a reasonable number of neuroses, but no body, no bowling average, and no obnoxious in-laws. A spirit will never die, unless subjected to extreme amounts of network television.

What do we mean when we say that God is self-existing?
When we say that God is self-existing we mean that when He plays creation games He is playing with Himself.

What do we mean when we say that God is infinitely perfect?
When we say that God is infinitely perfect, we are frankly just blowing smoke. God knows this, but doesn't make a big scene about it.

What are some of the perfections of God?
Some of the perfections of God are: God is all-good, all-knowing, all-present, almighty, all-conference, Allstate, all-purpose, and allspice. He also does incredible sunsets on the side.

If God is everywhere, why do we not see Him?
Although God is everywhere, we do not see him because for many years He has had big-dollar contracts with companies that pioneered stealth technology, such as Whamo and Goldman Sachs.

Does God see us?

Oh, He sees us all right—and watches over us with loving care. Imagine a power so great that He gets ten times better resolution than Google Earth Voyeur Edition—and that's on every planet in a trillion galaxies, give or take.

What is God's loving care for us called?

Many people call God's loving care for us "Divine Providence." Others prefer the term "surveillance."

Exercises

1) God can do all things because: (a) He has killer lobbyists; (b) He conducts frequent focus groups; (c) there are no other takers for a lot of the stuff He does; (e) Helen Mirren signed off on it.

2) God's care for us is called: (a) OCD; (b) meddling; (c) a behavioral experiment; (d) a violation of existing privacy laws.

3) Explain what Christ meant when he said, "Be ye perfect as My Father in Heaven is perfect." Was He egging you on in a hopeless effort? Was He suggesting that the Father maybe wasn't all *that* perfect? Or maybe just stirring up rivalry in the family? Compose your answer as a limerick.

LESSON 3

THE UNITY AND TRINITY OF GOD

"The trio with everlasting brio."

To Help You Get Through This Lesson

God has told us that in Himself there are three distinct Persons: the Father, the Son, and the Holy Ghost. Normally this would qualify Him as a Multiple Personality Poster Boy, but because He's God we can at least have the courtesy to listen. Just be sure not to invite Him to lunch—all three of Them show up and order a huge amount of food.

Each Person is God Almighty, yet they are *not* three Gods. They are exactly equal, metrically calibrated to eight or ten decimal places. None is older, nor greater, and none has a better Dun & Bradstreet rating than the others. The Son likes to thrash His fellow Persons at thumb wrestling, and the Holy Ghost enjoys destroying the Others at Scrabble, but in general They get along. They are *one* and the *same* God. To our tiny minds, this truth is a supernatural mystery, much like natural mysteries such as electricity or profitable restaurants, except that we can kind of understand the natural mysteries, whereas the Trinity we just have to accept as God's revelation, coming to us through a group of hugely wise old cross-dressers who favor full-length red watered-silk gowns.

How many Persons are there in God?
In God there are three Divine Persons—the Father, the Son, and the Holy Ghost. Applications have been submitted to allow a limited number of sub-divine positions within God and under the "God" brand, but so far the Original Persons have resisted expansion.

Are the three Divine Persons really distinct from one another?
The three Divine Persons are really distinct from one another. Though they're the same age, major distinctions in appearance are evident: the Son looks like He's taken much better care of Himself than has His Father—it's the difference between 40 days and 40 years of skin damage from intense desert sun.

The Holy Ghost is the little one with the beak and feathers.

Are the three Divine Persons perfectly equal to one another?
The three Divine Persons are perfectly equal to one another, right down to their views on same-sex marriage and the importance of precious metals in your portfolio. This is because They are all *one* and the *same* God. Seven or eight thousand years ago, the Divine Parity was certified by a leading Assyrian Umpire, but in modern times has been handled by the Price Waterhouse Spiritual Auditing Team, which beat out Accountants Without Borders to get the contract.

Can we fully understand how the three Divine Persons, though really distinct from one another, are one and the same God?

We just threw this in as a rhetorical question. Most people can't even remember their zip code.

Exercises

1) By the word "Divinity" we mean: (a) inhumanity; (b) Bette Midler fifteen years ago; (c) anyone really skilled at sports or acting; (d) a gooey kind of candy.

2) Even though we cannot understand how there are three Persons in God, we believe that there are because: (a) two would make them just an ordinary couple; (b) it just feels right; (c) doubting is such a downer; (d) survey says "three."

3) Discuss: Does God have the same number of natures as you do? Base your argument on the fact that no one really wants to get into a pissing match with God about anything.

LESSON 4

THE CREATION AND THE FALL OF MAN

"Wow, that looks delicious!"

To Help Get You Through This Lesson

Prototypes are messy, and that's a fact. It's as true of the first electric nose hair trimmer, originated in 1834 by The Shaker Image, a low-profile religious community with a huge mail order presence, as it is of the first crude beach towel, fashioned by David Hasselhoff in 1984. It was also true of God's experience with Adam and Eve, His 1.0 human beings. There is no glossing over the terrible debacle they were involved in, but let's stay positive here and deal cleanly with what the great Saint Anselm often called "a teleological shit storm."

Adam and Eve were slated to be showcase beings in God's Creation Portfolio, and He endowed them with all the goodies: looks, brains, and plenty of sanctifying grace, which they could trade for arcade tokens once they got to Heaven. They were a charismatic couple, living in a nudist paradise called the Garden of Eden. Though not married, they were very devoted to each other—and not just because there were no other mating choices.

So what went wrong? Well, for some reason, God decided to give them a little test, just to see if they were paying attention, being properly worshipful and all. It was a throwaway, a token self-control requirement involving eating issues. Wouldn't you know it would end up being about food?

They were told by God not to eat fruit from the Tree of Standard and Poor, yet they were tempted to do so by a talking reptile who told them it would give them the power to rate everything. Some have posited that the reptile was Rupert Murdoch, but persuasive evidence has been offered by many biblical scholars that it was actually Larry King. So the Godsy Twins ate the fruit, failed their test. They were then barred from the Garden of Eden, and, along with their descendants, made to endure all manner of pain, including self-consciousness, an inclination to sin, and needing to cover their private parts with fig leaves. This latter punishment would eventually lead to the even more excruciatingly painful phenomenon of the fashion industry.

Did God have Creator's Remorse? Very possibly. But even if God doesn't do regret at all, it is reasonable to wonder why He didn't take a mulligan, just dump His hand and get all new cards. Were these two geniuses really worth His Infinite Attention? Whatever the case, no one doubts that this epic tale of innocence, petty agricultural theft, betrayal, and redemption has all the makings of a great theocumentary, maybe with the help of M. Night Shyamalan.

But what is the take-home for you? The major item is: fair or not, you inherit Adam's problems in a condition called **original sin**. Maybe you don't get his hemorrhoids or his shingles, but you are guaranteed some of the basic forms of Adam-quality pain. You have to work. You have to accept sickness and suffering. You have to have relatives. You have to wait in line with your groceries while someone takes ten minutes to get a price check on the 24-ounce Swanson's frozen Flesh Sticks. And you have to die.

Also not terrific is the fact that you start out stupid and often end up that way, too. Thank the Lord that in such a wretched state most of you can still memorize Catechlysm answers.

What is man?

"Man" is a creature composed of body, soul, and a memory full of pop song lyrics. He is made in the image and likeness of God, though the resemblance isn't obvious most of the time. And don't forget that "man" is also "woman." For some reason, they want to be included in the whole mess.

Is this likeness to God in the body or in the soul?

The likeness couldn't be in the body, since God goes to the gym almost every day, and is not just All-Powerful, but All-Muscular and All-Chiseled, too. So the likeness must be in the soul. Do not strain yourself in the search.

Who were the first man and woman?

The first man and woman were Adam and Eve, the parents of the whole human race and the only people whose immediate family engaged in widespread and completely defensible incest.

What gifts were bestowed on Adam and Eve by God?

The gifts bestowed on Adam and Eve by God were sanctifying grace, fun times in the Garden of Eden, freedom from suffering and death, fitted sheets, and a really beautiful espresso maker.

What has happened to us on account of the sin of Adam?

On account of the sin of Adam, we, his descendants, come into the world more or less doomed. Not to be too negative about it, of course. But we do arrive without sanctifying grace or any invisible means of support whatsoever. We inherit Adam's punishment, just as we would have inherited his gifts had he been obedient to God. Just as the child of a prison inmate is automatically thrown into jail when he is born, or like the child of a bishop becomes a cleric at birth. Like that.

What is this sin in us called?

This sin is called "original sin" by some. Others call it "guilt by association."

Is God unjust in punishing us on account of the sin of Adam?

Of course not. Being All-Powerful, God can do whatever He wants. He owns the game and the rules, and He is not taking away anything to which we have a strict right as human beings. Punishing all of us *does* seem just a tad ungracious, and appears on the surface to lack qualities of love and mercy. But then He created those, too. And anyway, you do not want to take on the celestial legal team in a protracted court battle—they'll eat you alive.

Was any human being ever preserved from original sin?

Some historians believe that the sixth century anchorite Saint Polygrip was preserved from original sin, citing as evidence his happy-go-lucky nature and his ability to eat corn on the cob well into his eighties. The names of Oscar Wilde and Joan of Arc have also come up in this context, but the only name which most heavily-indoctrinated Catholics put squarely into this category is that of the Blessed Virgin Mary. She was preserved from original sin in view of the merits of her Divine Son, and that privilege was called her Immaculate Conception. Though there are no records, scholars assume that her parents, Joachim and Anne, "knew each other" in more or less normal fashion, further deepening the beauty of this mystery.

Exercises

1) God's chief gift to Adam and Eve was: (a) rent-free living; (b) a visit to the reptile petting zoo; (c) two hours a day of self time, away from Him; (d) a sense of humor.

2) Every child born today has an inclination to: (a) cheat; (b) Type II Diabetes; (c) get a bad tattoo; (d) grow up.

3) Project: Notice how many things you have to do that you find hard, that you would have found easy to do if Adam and Eve had not sinned. Write them down and bring them to class tomorrow. Keep it to 100 items maximum. Do not simply write the word "Everything" and turn it in. Be sure to list having to do this idiot project.

LESSON 5

THE INCARNATION

"The Word was made Flesh, and
within two weeks was being sold
with fries and a Coke for $3.99."

To Help You Get Through This Lesson

So after the Adam and Eve catastrophe, things looked
pretty bleak for Team Humanity. God was All-Annoyed
with us, and Satan was never on our side to begin with. If
it were a soccer match, humanity would be the ball.

But in this lesson you will learn there was hope. God
promised Adam He would stay in touch. No firm date, you
understand, but for people who had just discovered that
to survive they were going to have to kill large vicious animals with sharp sticks, God's words were comforting. He
told them that someday he would send His Divine Son,
Jesus Christ, to be the Savior of all people. His mission
would be to **free man from his sins** and to **reopen
the gates of Heaven**. Though this wasn't exactly what
humanity wanted to hear, they were polite about it. No
point in asking for propane stoves and chemical toilets if
it's just going to get God all revved up again.

Finally, at the end of the Old Testament—right after
the Book of Malachi—God sent an angel to the Blessed
Virgin Mary of Nazareth to ask her to be the mother of

God's Son. Without much haggling, she agreed to a deal, details of which were never disclosed. The power of the Holy Spirit came over her and Jesus was immediately conceived—half-God, half-man, 100 percent Messiah. Obviously so, since the Holy Spirit, Third Person of the Trinity, is not going to shoot blanks.

This was the **Incarnation**, which culminated in the birth of Jesus in Bethlehem on Christmas Day. You need to remember that Mary was truly God's mom, but that her husband Joseph was not the father. He was the guardian of Jesus, or, as French people often referred to such a person in those days, *un cocu*.

You should also remember that though current theological authorities readily accept these events, some experts question the less-than-robust response of God in the face of the Adam and Eve mess. If mankind was doomed to so much overwhelming pain and suffering, and was obviously in need of serious redemption, why send just *one* Savior? Current thinking holds that Operation Messiah was important enough, and the planet large enough, to warrant the use of overwhelming force to get the redemptive job done. Shock and Awe were clearly required. Figures have been bandied about in reference to the needs of such a campaign, and the consensus of the experts is that anywhere from 180 to 300 Messiahs would have been needed to get an acceptable level of salvation in all parts of the world. Their distribution has also been hotly debated, but the generally accepted numbers include 60 to 70 Messiahs in the populous Middle East and North African areas, roughly the same number in the Far East, and 30 to 40 for the other major land masses. Isolated as it was even then, Australia would receive Messiahs on an availability basis.

Did God abandon man after Adam fell into sin?

To be honest, at first Adam was a little worried that God had lost his contact information, since the silence was chilly after so much *bonhomie* in the Garden; but no, God did not abandon Adam but promised to send into the world a Savior to free man from his sins, to reopen the gates of Heaven, and to get the economy moving again.

What is the chief teaching of the Catholic Church about Jesus Christ?

The chief teaching of the Catholic Church about Jesus Christ is that He is God made man, the Savior of humanity, and should be worshipped with fervor but also with dignity, and *not* by doing nutty stuff like falling to the floor and rolling around, or shouting gibberish in the middle of a service, or by handling venomous snakes.

Why is Jesus Christ God?

Along with everyone else, we are just not sure on this one. Maybe He was just a member of the "Lucky Big Bang Club," who knows?

Why is Jesus Christ man?

Probably because He didn't want to have to go through all the shit women deal with every day.

Is Jesus Christ more than one person?

Jesus Christ is the Second Person of the Blessed Trinity, period. What, you think He should be more than that?

How was the Son of God made man?

This is a technical issue, beyond the scope of the Catechlysm. It is a private matter, between the Holy Spirit, the Blessed Virgin, and their fertility specialist.

When was the Son of God conceived and made man?
The Son of God was conceived and made man on Annunciation Day, the day on which the Angel Gabriel found the Blessed Virgin Mary hiding behind a potted palm, trying to look as much like a palm frond as possible, and announced to her that she was to be the Mother of God.

When was Christ born?
Christ's timing was great: He was born on Christmas Day, in Bethlehem, just in time for the busiest retail season of the year. The three kings took advantage of terrific discounts to bring Him some stunning gifts.

Exercises

1) After Adam sinned, God in His mercy promised to send: (a) condolences; (b) him to obedience school; (c) a Quizno's gift card; (d) instructions for building a fire.

2) When Christ became man, He did not lose His: (a) dignity; (b) ethereal good looks; (c) right to judge all of us; (d) ability to do a hilarious sea lion imitation.

3) Discuss: Did God force Mary to become the Mother of Christ? Be sure to include possible issues of coercion, unwanted attention, etc. You will need to address the idea that if Mary said no, it would be a perfect waste of the only Immaculate Conception in existence, and God would be obliged to create another one, which would take time. Examine His Old Testament record for patience and forbearance, but don't be too hard on Him.

LESSON 6

THE REDEMPTION

"You're only as guilty as you feel!"

To Help You Get Through This Lesson

Obviously, this redemption is not about frequent flier miles or gift premiums from American Express. The headline here is: Christ died for our sins. By allowing Himself to be nailed to a wooden cross, He became the sacrifice that **redeemed** us from the sin of Adam and Eve. He got our spiritual car out of the impound lot, so we suddenly have the right to be children of God and attain Heaven as long as we meet the tough admissions criteria.

As if that weren't enough, He then came *back to life* three days after the Crucifixion, and emerged from His tomb to present Himself to His astounded followers, proving that even death itself was His bitch.

This is a very big deal. In fact, it's probably *the* biggest deal in a religion known for a yearly calendar crammed with feast days celebrating miraculous events, brilliant thinkers, berserko ascetics, and spectacularly bloody martyrs.

Because the Crucifixion/Redemption is so huge and uber-solemn for all Catholics, you will eventually have to face the big questions: Just how guilty are you? How much do you owe God for this Redemption? In the

Church's deep past, these questions drove untold numbers of the faithful to whip themselves with fan belts from old cars, and to fast until their stomachs were the size of Reese's Peanut Butter Cups; luckily for all of us, this is no longer the case. The world changed for all believers in the summer of 1991, when a near-capacity crowd of over 600,000 gathered in the Jerry Lewis Farce-o-Drome in Fontainebleau, France, for International Youth Guilt Day. It was there that Pope John Paul II joined Doctor Phil on stage and electrified the crowd with his now famous words: "You are all just so obviously guilty! Guilty of Christ's death! Guilty of not loving Him enough! Guilty of sins that are like spitting in His face! But hear me now, all of you! Just because you're guilty doesn't mean you can't be *happy* and have *fun*. That's right. The Church's new position is: God is a grown-up. If He chose to sacrifice Himself for us, we take that as a *freely offered* sacrifice, which comes with no expectations of us on His part, no fine print, no ridiculous attempt to guilt us into behaving like polite robots. We believe that God takes responsibility for His actions, and is not acting out like some sour grandparent who says, 'And after all I've done for you, this is how you repay me?' That is absurd, and we reject it for all time, definitively, *ex cathedra*, and no take-backsies!"

It was even better hearing him say this with that paprika-laden accent of his.

So, having dumped that terrible load, you can now appreciate this lesson and its description of the last fifty days of Christ's itinerary on Earth. A couple of items to remember as you go through it: one, *limbo* is a metaphysical location and not a party game; and two, if we are terribly wrong about God being a grown-up and He turns out to be just plain pissed at everyone when He comes back to judge all of us, please recall that we were never officially in agreement with the Pope and his nutty ideas.

What is meant by the Redemption?

If you've been Dempted once already, and you're over twenty-one so your Demption cannot be expunged from the records, you will generally still get two warnings before your Redemption. But once it happens, you have no one to blame but yourself.

What were the chief sufferings of Christ?

The chief sufferings of Christ were His agony in the Garden of Gethsemane, His cruel scourging, His death on the cross, His terrible foreboding that deep-fried Twinkies would become a popular snack food, and His realization that a plunge into the depths of most human souls would hardly get His feet wet.

When did Christ die?

He died when He was no longer breathing. We don't have an exact time of death because Luke, his attending physician, was not able to be present due to a previous engagement with self-preservation.

What do we learn from the sufferings and death of Christ?

We learn what it means to have the bejabbers scared out of us. Or if not, we learn to tune out the whole story as too confusing and depressing, and not as interesting as Wonder Woman, Spider-Man, or Magnum, P.I.

What do we mean when we say in the Apostles' Creed that Christ descended into Hell?

When we say that Christ descended into Hell, we do *not* mean that He made a visit to Alabama. This "descent" was actually a quick meet-and-greet in "limbo," a place of quiet, calm, tedious rest, where Christ created quite a noise while visiting with the souls of the just who were waiting for Him there. Most of these had been forced to wait a century or more to attain Heaven and were feeling cranky at the long line and lack of clean restrooms. He expedited the paperwork of all present, except for the few who were tossed back into Purgatory for their snarky, potty-mouth remarks about preferring a thousand years in a Greyhound Bus Station.

When did Christ rise from the dead?
When you're the Second Person of the Blessed Trinity, you pretty much rise from the dead whenever you want. In this case, Christ selected the Sunday following His crucifixion, in many ways an unfortunate choice. It turned out to be Easter Sunday, when people were already preoccupied with big department store free-for-alls, Easter egg hunts, and preparations of huge ham dinners with pineapple rings, maraschino cherries, and sweet, sticky sauces. Church historians are convinced in retrospect that His glorious Resurrection would have garnered more press had the date been more carefully chosen.

Why did Christ rise from the dead?
If you consider the alternative, wouldn't you rather? And if you have God's perfect mastery of cellular regeneration, it's a no-brainer.

When did Christ ascend into Heaven?
Christ ascended—body and soul, sandals and tunic, loose change and breath mints—into Heaven on Ascension Day, forty days after His Resurrection.

Why did Christ remain on Earth forty days after His Resurrection?

Unless you yourself have created a religion, you cannot imagine all the work involved, even after you're dead. *Especially* after you're dead. In Christ's case, He felt He had to prove that He was truly risen from the dead (though that does carry a little whiff of insecurity), and then there were the million-and-one details He had to be sure the Apostles understood, such as which of them get to wear the pointy hats, who gets to sit in the big chair in the middle of the room, and who gets to eat the really big communion wafer with all the decorations on it.

What do we mean when we say that Christ will come from his place at the right hand of the Father to judge the living and the dead?

What we mean is that on the Last Day, when Earth will have become unlivable through the effects of climate change, high doses of Ben and Jerry's in the ground water, and an overload of forgettable, derivative music, Our Lord will come to pronounce a sentence of eternal reward or eternal punishment on everyone who has ever lived in this world. For those of you who know you will need a false passport and cosmetic surgery, our advice is to get on it ASAP. Practice your Meekness. And bring something to eat. As fast as Our Lord normally works, the caseload is formidable and there will be periodic interruptions when all the breast implants in the world explode with a thunderous crack, and horned beasts and other apparitions create multitudes of rubberneckers.

Exercises

1) Christ undid the harm done to the human race by another man whose name was: (a) redacted by God the

Father's editing team; (b) Rod Blagojevich; (c) Silvio Berlusconi; (d) protected by privacy laws.

2) Discuss: God planned the death of His Son, yes, but why was the scenario so Old Testament and heavy-handed? When the Lord sayeth vengeance was His, did He mean to use that vengeance against His Son, for some reason? Be frank, but do not invite a lightning strike.

3) Our sins not only offend God but they are really the reasons for all natural disasters, rampant homosexuality everywhere but in the priesthood, and the suffering and death of Christ. Write the words of a prayer in which you tell God what you as His loving child think of sin and what you will do about sin in the future. A little indignation is appropriate, and a light sycophantic touch, but no salty language and no graphic descriptions of violence. And don't make promises you can't keep. God can detect histrionics and phony bravado from light years away. Remember, He wasn't born yesterday—He always was and always will be.

LESSON 7

THE HOLY GHOST AND GRACE

"I believe in the Holy Ghost, but . . . a *bird*?"

To Help Get You Through This Lesson

The Holy Ghost, represented by a dove, has always dwelt in the Church. Which is why your steps have that unmistakable dry-guano crunchiness as you walk down the nave. The role of the Holy Ghost has always been to give life to the Church and sanctify it, making it an environment that is holy as well as nitrogen-rich. The Holy Ghost also sanctifies all Church members by providing sanctifying grace that pours down on the faithful, giving them a share in the life of God Himself, as well as some brutal dry-cleaning bills.

Besides sanctifying grace, there are two other kinds of grace provided by the Holy Ghost: actual grace, which is okay and very helpful if the sanctifying variety is temporarily out of stock. It helps you overcome your abysmal ignorance and your well-known inclination to evil, both of which have been heavily documented by your family and friends. Lastly, there is snackifying grace, which comes to the aid of those who are afflicted with the habit of trying to fill their internal spiritual void with between-meal noshes. This grace miraculously leads them to the nearest vending machine, where they can attain temporary paradise, becoming one with some Funyuns or Hostess Ding Dongs.

You should be aware that historically the Holy Ghost has had an image problem. It's hard being a bird, even a small graceful one, when you're in the company of God the Father and His Son. Those of us who are old enough to remember have already forgotten the 1891 call-in radio show on WREK in Pigeon, West Virginia, that asked listeners for suggestions on rebranding the Holy Ghost to boost His profile vis-à-vis the Other Two Persons of the Trinity. We have vague memories of names like the Holy Shade, the Holy Spook, the Holy Specter, and the Holy Phantom being bandied about. No one liked "the Holy Poltergeist."

At any rate, whether you call Him the Sacred Wraith or the Holy Spirit, the dove has trouble garnering respect. It *is* a little suspicious, too, that right up front the Apostles' Creed allots so much space to the Father and the Son, and mentions the Holy Ghost only toward the end, as part of the laundry list that the faithful glide over quickly in the race to "Amen."

Whether or not the complete silence of the Holy Ghost reminds you of Harpo Marx, you are well-advised to remember that this dove is truly God, and in speaking of Him you should go light on references to chocolate or moisturizing soap.

Who is the Holy Ghost?
The Holy Ghost is God, the Third Person of the Blessed Trinity. He's kind of like a profane ghost, but with extraordinarily powerful associates and the ability to saturate the major capital markets with sanctifying grace.

From whom does the Holy Ghost proceed?

The answer we received from the Ecclesiastical Copy Writing Department is, "The Holy Ghost proceeds from the Father and the Son," but attorneys for the Holy Ghost have rejected this language, on grounds that it might imply "third-among-equals" status for Him. In any case, they feel that the writing is perilously close to gibberish—though to be fair, they haven't yet seen the New Revised Catechlysm.

Is the Holy Ghost equal to the Father and the Son?

Of course. The fact that you're *asking* is a little off-putting. Is this more "Diss the Dove"?

Can we resist the grace of God?

We don't know about *you*, but *we* can't. Even though we have free will and all that, grace is so scrumptious that normally God just has to dangle some of it in front of us, and we give in to temptation right away. We always feel so cheap later on.

Is actual grace necessary for all who have attained the use of reason?

Yes, actual grace is necessary for all who have attained the use of reason, because without it we cannot long resist the power of temptation. But let's face it: actual grace is needed even more among the much larger demographic that lives on beef jerky and Monster Loca-Moca drink, and who can't locate their own navels.

What are the principal ways of obtaining grace?

The principal ways of obtaining grace are: receiving the sacraments, prayer, cajoling, wheedling, weeping, coaxing, and pleading. Flattery and humor work sometimes, too.

Exercises

1) The Third Person of the Blessed Trinity is: (a) crazy about sunflower seeds; (b) a star of behavioral psychology; (c) hard to remember; (d) a little flighty.

2) Any gift of God can be called: (a) an eBay moneymaker; (b) pretty righteous; (c) a *quid pro quo*; (d) a return for store credit.

3) Since grace is the life of Christ in the soul, we must imitate Christ in order to lead this life. Let each boy and girl make a poster, diagram, cartoon, music video, flash mob, or full-length feature depicting a practical way in which a modern boy or girl can imitate an action or virtue in the life of Christ. Be sure to steer clear of changing water into wine, walloping money changers in the temple, walking on water, calming storms, raising the dead, curing lepers or blind persons, driving demons into a herd of swine, inexplicably multiplying food products, having meals with prostitutes, perspiring blood, being flogged and crucified for the sins of others, rising from the dead, and ascending bodily into Heaven. Other than those—go for it. No limits!

LESSON 8

I BELIEVE . . . IN THE

HOLY CATHOLIC CHURCH

"Thou art Peter, and upon this rock-like cranium I will place a stunning triple tiara."

To Help You Get Through This Lesson

The Church is the congregation of all baptized persons united in the **same true faith**, the same sacrifice, the same sacraments, with the same prejudices, the same denial, the same hypocrisy, and the same impressive array of fears. (Some latitude is permitted in table manners, personal grooming, and facial expressions.) The congregation has always been under the authority of the same kind of male, autocratic Pope, with the exception of a few confusing moments in history when apparently there were two Popes, and briefly a woman Pope. Some of our editors seem to recall a plow horse and an egret as Popes, but these people have inhaled the fumes of too much printer's ink, and are not entirely reliable.

Jesus Christ founded the Church to **save all of humanity** by providing the kind of structured play that allows for psychological growth and personal enrichment. Wait, hold it. No—that's the Waldorf Schools. But the Church did fine work, too. It provided a solid belief system, with a resulting self-righteousness that over many centuries engendered not just widespread abuse of power within the organization, but extraordinarily thorough persecution of virtually all those outside it.

This was possible because of the Holy Ghost's presence in the Church, which gave it life and bestowed on it the ability to teach, sanctify, rule, and generally mess with its members as it consistently claims Christ wishes it to do.

It is impossible to overstate the power and influence (or, in Italian, *influenza*) of the Church in the cultural life of the western world. The great themes of the Bible and of the Church's mission have found sublime expression in countless art works down through the centuries, from Michelangelo's Sistine Chapel fresco, "Pull My Finger," to Leonardo da Vinci's celebrated work "The Last Color-by-Numbers Supper."

Even in recent history, the Church's influence is everywhere. Few people realize that the idea for McDonald's franchise signs which carry the "total sold" message was ripped off from the Church and its Grosso Totals Board, which has been in Saint Peter's square for centuries, and now reads: "Roman Catholic Church—over 800 billion souls saved."

What is the Church?
The Church is a red-hot multinational operation based in Rome, and is a huge player in the trillion-dollar international religion industry. Each year, through the efforts of its COO, the Holy Ghost, it churns out huge quantities of masses, sacraments, prayers, and indulgences, both off-the-rack and the more upscale tailored-to-fit, all of which generate revenues estimated to be in the hundreds of billions. Exact figures are not available, since the Church is not obliged by law to open its books, it being a privately-

held corporation wholly owned by the Blessed Trinity, Incorporated.

Who founded the Church?

Jesus Christ founded the Church with seed money from a local farmer. In an initially difficult financial environment, some of the seed money was choked off by a freeze-up of the inter-bank lending system, and some of it withered from having landed in CDs with miserable interest rates. Luckily, some fell on fertile ground and ended up in sweetheart deals with monarchs, or with tax-free status in various republics, allowing it to thrive and yield bountiful dividends, yea, unto a hundredfold.

Why did Jesus Christ found the Church?

Jesus Christ founded the Church because He was suddenly seized by the Entrepreneurial Spirit, and saw a chance to make a killing while bringing all men to eternal salvation. As the Confraternity of the Firesign Theatre put it in one of their many works on the subject of a loving and avaricious God, "Just because you're surrounded by evil doesn't mean you can't make some money from it."

When was the dwelling of the Holy Ghost in the Church first visibly manifested?

The dwelling of the Holy Ghost in the Church was first visibly manifested on Pentecost Sunday, when He visited the Apostles in the form of tongues of fire. In the event, their headquarters building burned to the ground, and the insurance company's inquest asked a lot of testy questions about why He couldn't just show up as a dove, as He usually did. The settlement the Apostles finally received covered expenses for their first half-dozen preaching missions, a sprinkler system, and new sandals for everyone.

How long will the Holy Ghost dwell in the Church?

We are told He will dwell in the Church until the end of time, but frankly His tenure will depend more on how robust the international regulatory agencies are in pursuing their respective mandates.

To whom did Christ give the power to teach, to sanctify, and to mess with the members of His Church?

Christ gave the power to teach, to sanctify, and to mess with the members of His Church to the Apostles, the first sales executives of the Church.

Did Christ give special power in His Church to any one of the Apostles?

Christ, in His infinite savvy, gave special power to Saint Peter by making him head of the Apostles and ruler of the entire Church. This was done to prevent any kind of runaway power grab, since Peter was generally acknowledged to be too thick to do anything genuinely aggressive or dangerous. What nobody counted on was the appearance of that guy Saul, or Paul, or whatever.

Who assists the bishops, as successors to the Apostles, in the care of souls?

Depending on the type of assistance required, the bishops are assisted by parish priests, by generous parishioners with equally generous bank accounts, or by young, comely, enthusiastic males who are called subdeacons, acolytes, gofers, or sometimes just "cutie," by the bishops and priests.

Exercises

1) Christ's representative on Earth is: (a) subject to feelings of inferiority; (b) always invited to Silvio Berlusconi's get-togethers; (c) constantly practicing humility; (d) charming but purely decorative.

2) If we hurt a member of the Church, we hurt: (a) whichever of our hands we punched him with; (b) the bottom line; (c) a customer; (d) our chances to be saved.

3) The special power that Christ gave to Saint Peter, which he has passed down to all the Popes who have succeeded him is: (a) being able to maintain a year-round tan; (b) complete freedom from nasal hair; (c) the ability to induce obedience in others; (d) the power to guess anyone's weight, within two pounds; (e) the ability to be nice almost all the time.

LESSON 9

THE COMMUNION OF SAINTS AND

FORGIVENESS OF SINS

"Oh how I long to be in that number, when the Saints com-mun-i-on!"

To Help Get You Through This Lesson

Think of the Communion of Saints as an unconventional convention, a get-together of three groups that can never get together. It's a little paradoxical, yes, but once you understand the theological points, it's going to seem almost sensible.

The Communion of Saints (COMMOSA) includes first and foremost the **blessed in Heaven,** headed up by Blessed General George Paten, who reports directly to Christ; second, the **faithful members of the Church on Earth**; and third, the **souls in Purgatory**. All are referred to as "saints" in a euphemistic way, much like NASCAR fans are addressed as "Ladies and Gentlemen."

Important for you to remember: the Communion of Saints is a more exclusive group than anybody realizes, because the membership is smaller than what you might expect. For example, there are really only 3,132 souls in Heaven, down from 3,133, before Saint Christopher was adjudged never to have existed. Purgatory, where souls go for a fiery but cleansing touch-up prior to heading for Heaven, has a more robust population of 11,488, but most of them are paying residual dues on so much sin that it'll take millennia before most of them see their last live ember. The number of Church faithful on Earth—we mean the truly faithful—is much more difficult to track, what with aggressive missionary work in Africa pumping the numbers up, while increasing numbers of women getting post-graduate degrees and using birth control works as a counter-trend. The 2010 report from the Rand Corporation puts the number somewhere between 5,000 and 850,000, leaning toward the higher number if you include baptized souls who are a little shaky about their belief in the Virgin Birth, who can't remember the words to any prayers, or who are frustrated that Christ didn't just fry the Romans with lightning bolts and establish an eternal kingdom of righteousness and justice when He had the chance.

Everybody knows where the growth is, of course. There are always bad jokes going around COMMOSA about having to add another wing onto Hell, or about its generous clerical discount.

What the constituent parts of COMMOSA do together is what groups have been doing for each other since the first Rotarian crawled out of the primordial ooze and led a class in prayer breakfast networking: *they help each other.*

The souls in Purgatory are helpless, much like customers at the DMV or the post office: they don't have much to do but stand in line, burning and waiting and suffering. But on the bright side, they give those in Heaven a reason to stay active. Heavenly residents don't need anything from anyone of course, since they're in Heaven, but through prayer they can help purgatorials—and earthlings too. Maybe get a particularly hot coal off the duodenum of a soul in Purgatory who is feeling like the thing has been there for an eternity. Maybe help an earthling get exact change for the Laundromat. Now that they're in Heaven it's perfectly normal they should want to give something back. Not too much, but something.

Earthlings, known as the panhandlers of the universe, will take any kind of help from anyone in COMMOSA, including God, and it is generally agreed that whatever it is—they need it.

Though the saints in Heaven admit it's an eternal struggle to keep earthlings in the contest for salvation, they agree that God was All-Brilliant when He came up with the idea of giving the Church **the power to forgive all sins on Earth**, every time, as often as necessary. This model was adopted after it became evident that the faithful on Earth were almost uniformly capable of highly creative, breathtaking, seemingly endless sinning.

Through the Communion of Saints, what can the blessed in Heaven do for the souls in Purgatory and the faithful on Earth?

With the tremendous amount of pull they have with the Trinity, the blessed in Heaven can always do some heavy lifting for those in Purgatory and on Earth. This is done mostly through prayer, since AT&T has an exclusive contract as Heaven's cell network provider and reception is terrible. The biggest obstacle to even greater help for those in Purgatory and on Earth is the lack of motivation on the part of the blessed. They truly *want* to help, but when you are finally there, in Heaven, with entrance to all attractions covered for eternity, maintaining focus on the little people becomes extremely challenging.

Should the faithful on Earth, through the Communion of Saints, honor the blessed in Heaven and pray to them?

Are you kidding? Of course! Doing a messy, inconsistent job of honoring and praying to the blessed in Heaven is worse than butt-dialing your mother from an all-night party.

What is meant in the Apostles' Creed by "the forgiveness of sins"?

By "the forgiveness of sins" in the Apostles' Creed is meant that God has given the Church serious leverage with sinners. The Church has them by the short hairs of their pubic tonsure because sinners know they can *always* count on being forgiven for the most wretched sins, but only if they confess them to a priest and appear remorseful (see "Penance" in Part III for tips on doing this convincingly). So the good news is they can continue to make a mess out of their lives over and over, with impunity. The bad news is they can continue to make a mess out of their lives over and over, with impunity.

Exercises

1) The souls in Purgatory want our prayers and: (a) an iced tea; (b) our car keys; (c) the right to unionize; (d) a chance to explain.

2) The best way to help others is: (a) to learn to dance; (b) never obvious; (c) to get adequate sex every day; (d) to underachieve.

3) To be effective, prayer must always be joined to: (a) political aspirations; (b) a chance to win valuable prizes; (c) dark motives; (d) a decent soundtrack.

LESSON 10

THE RESURRECTION AND

LIFE EVERLASTING

"Amen, amen I say to you, like Crazy Bread from Little Caesar's, we shall all indeed rise."

To Help Get You Through This Lesson

When you die, you're going to notice a few things. One, the picture on your flat-screen lacks crispness. Two, the hospice attendant is sitting down, drinking a Mountain Dew and looking a little relieved. Three, you peed in your bed. And that terrible smell? It's you.

Immediately after that, when your soul and body decide that a separation would be best, you will undergo the **particular judgment** by Christ. Above all, don't be thrown by the fact that He's a little formal and distant. Remember that He's your Savior and He loves you very much, but He's just doing His job. What could go wrong?

Okay, a few things. To be honest, we wouldn't count on ducking right under the velvet ropes and getting to see God immediately. That kind of purity and sanctifying grace at the end of a life is rare; it hasn't been seen since the deaths of Mother Teresa in 1997 and Jack Palance in 2006. More realistically, you should shoot to be one of those basically stand-up people who is a little tarnished by venial sin but has a heart of semiprecious metal, like a movie character played by Marisa Tomei. Rather than being one of the Damned, you will be among the Darned. You will have to spend, say, eight or nine hundred years in the flames of Purgatory, but finally you get to see the face of God forever. If you're not the self-conscious type, it is complete paradise.

Then there is Hell. Though Hell was originally a parlor game used by the Numidian oligarchy around 200 B.C. to abuse prisoners of war, God managed to option it soon after that, outbidding both the Hohenzollern family and Atari Games. After a few roughish, disappointing prototypes were adjudged too lenient and cushy, the current version was put in place. Unfortunately, it has been a huge success, easily the biggest program currently operating in Creation.

As reverent students of this slim volume, you do not need to be told to avoid Hell like a meal at Applebee's.

But if, despite the sage instructions we offer, you find yourself standing before Christ without a drop of sanctifying grace in your hip flask, and mortal sins smeared on your face like Taco Bell Nachos Bellgrande on a drunk at 3 a.m., then woe unto you, as the Bible is fond of saying. Your soul ends up out of the presence of God, roasting in unquenchable flames, *forever*. That's right—much longer even than the perceived running time of any single Academy Awards ceremony in history.

What then happens to your body? That question brings us to the topic of the **general judgment**. You see, after you die your body decomposes, very much like a Sarah Palin speech under scrutiny; but when the End of the World arrives, when the trumpets blow, when all of the world's remaining water beds are torn asunder, then the bodies of all those who have died are reunited with their souls. Presumably reconstituted in some way, though the process is strictly proprietary and not for us to know. (Just add water? Amino acids? Beef tea?)

With just the right touch of anticlimax in honor of the Antichrist, all body-soul combinations then continue with the happiness or suffering they had been appreciating theretofore only as a soul. (Or "soulo", as the most thoroughly damned might put it.) All we can say by way of consolation to the Hell-bound is that the rumors about rotisserie spits inserted in various orifices are unsubstantiated.

What is meant by "the resurrection of the body"?

To be clear, this has absolutely nothing to do with any episode of "CSI—End of Days." By "the resurrection of the body" is meant that at the End of the World the bodies of all people will rise from the Earth and be united again to their souls. Huge disappointment is expected on the part of the souls, because so many of the bodies really will have let themselves go, shamefully. Some attempts at trades will be inevitable. Walt Disney's suit will need pressing, and he'll have a little freezer burn here and there, but he will be one of the few to have an easy reunification.

Why will the bodies of the just rise?

The bodies of the just will rise in order to showcase the finest soul/body specimens headed for Heaven. As we have pointed out, God is All-Savvy when it comes to public relations, and he would not miss a once-in-eternity opportunity like this one. As Saint John Bosco said when he was appointed captain of the 1842 Papal Olympic Gymnastics Team: "God grant these beautiful boys recognition on the Olympic podium and later at the general judgment. Photos and video by permission only!"

Why will the bodies of the damned also rise?

The bodies of the damned also rise, but as part of a cooperative effort between the World Health Organization (WHO) and the International Environment Program Trust (INEPT), working with heavenly forces in treating the Earth as a kind of supernatural superfund site. Protocols will be in place to see that, as the damned are reconstituted, Christ performs a strict triage, separating their horribly polluted bodies and souls not just from those who might be offended by the smell, but from the Earth itself. Original plans called for relocating the damned to the prairies of west Texas, but after intercession by the mother of Christ it was decided to move them to Hell, on humanitarian grounds.

If everyone is judged immediately after death, why will there be a general judgment?

Although everyone is judged immediately after death, it is fitting that there be a general judgment in order that God's justice, wisdom, and mercy should be on display before the awards banquet, which will be staged to recognize all those who worked so hard over the millennia to make human life so much fun and the great success that it was. Thanks especially to the Holy Ghost for a fantastic no-host bar.

What are the rewards or punishments appointed for humanity after the particular judgment?

Rewards are limited to one: Heaven. Any complaints about lack of selection in the rewards program will qualify the whiner for one of the substantial array of punishments. These include: Purgatory, for the quasi-bad, or Darned, those who were without a really convincing life of sin and who will eventually gain Heaven after being roasted to perfection like an espresso bean; Hell, for hard-core evildoers who commit two mortal sins before getting out of bed in the morning and who apparently don't mind spending a long stretch of time deprived of the vision of God and suffering dreadful torments; lastly, there is working at a casino in Las Vegas, essentially the same as Hell but with more smoke in the air and 24/7 gambling available.

Exercises

1) Those who die in mortal sin have no chance to: (a) wear white after Labor Day; (b) stain their reputations a little more; (c) try out the cup holders on the celestial limousines; (d) continue breathing.

2) Being obedient is one way to lessen the need for: (a) freedom; (b) the lash; (c) pharmaceuticals in the drinking water; (d) trips to the bathroom.

3) Project: Fifty times, copy the words of the "Ejaculation" found in the front of the Catechlysm. It is an excellent prayer to say as you go to sleep every night with the thought of death in mind.

PART II

THE COMMANDMENTS OF GOD

LESSON 11

THE TWO GREAT COMMANDMENTS

It's true that the word "commandment" can be a little off-putting. I mean, is it like the Church is *commanding* you to do something? Are they ordering you to do it?

Yeah, pretty much. But the Church doesn't want you to obey the Commandments like some kind of slave. In this day and age, you have to get in there and bargain a little, do some negotiating. We'll show you what we mean.

Let's look at the Two Great Commandments, so named because though they were articulated by Jesus Christ, they were adapted from a story treatment by Alexander the Great (and thus his right to a title credit), and because they led directly to the Great Depression, which in turn led to the invention of Anti-Depressants:

1. Thou shalt love the Lord thy God with thy whole heart, with thy whole soul, and with thy whole mind, and with thy whole strength.
2. Thou shalt love thy neighbor as thyself.

So you go to your parish priest to have a sensible chat about this stuff. A social call, nothing too heavy. You might want to get your mom to buy a bottle of whiskey you can give him. Nothing too good, though: maybe a bottle of Four Roses. These guys go through it like water, and they can't tell the difference anyway. Okay, so what you *don't* want to do is come right out and say "Screw it, I can't do this stuff, I don't even know what the hell you mean." This just makes everybody defensive. Your opening position on the First Great Commandment is: Look, most days the whole "soul and strength and mind and heart" thing is just too much for me. Hey, I'm just a kid! What do you say to 30 percent of the soul and strength, and 40 percent of the mind and heart? Consistently, rain or shine, like clockwork. That's not chopped liver, right? And when you're through with the discussion, and he's made a good dent in the bottle, you come out in all four categories at, say, 50 percent during the week, and maybe in the 60s on Sunday. Something everybody can live with.

The Second Great Commandment is a little touchier, but nothing that can't be managed. It does involve a little finessing of the truth, though. Say something like, "Can I fill your glass, Father? I gotta be honest with you here: I have self-esteem issues. And since I don't like myself much, I feel like I'm going to be short-changing my neighbor by treating him the same crappy way I treat myself. How about if I just try to stay out of everyone's way, but do it in God's name so it's official and everything?"

Exercises

1) God gave the Ten Commandments to Moses on Mount Sinai. He wrote the Commandments with His own finger on two tablets of stone. Which finger did He use? And what does He recommend for nail care after something like this?

2) Catherine helped another girl, who was tired, to wash dishes and to run errands. On her way home she helped a blind man to cross the street. How could Catherine make these ordinary deeds true works of mercy, other than by stopping her terrible tendency to en-

able everyone around her, and instead let them fend for themselves, thus learning valuable lessons? (Extra credit: Google "Ayn Rand" and write a denunciation of Catherine based on Rand's ideas.)

SPECIAL SECTION
FOR SELECT, ELITE STUDENTS ONLY
(MANDATORY READING FOR ALL)

This is about what we call the "Evangelical Counsels," which is just a fancy way of saying good sound advice coming direct to you from God—through Jesus, through the New Testament of the Bible, then through His Church and landing here in the pages of your New Revised Catechylsm.

So what is God telling you now? What's His advice? He's advising you to be all that you can be. He's saying that negotiating your way through the Two Great Commandments is okay, but it doesn't make you the Rock Star you want to be, deep down. What you really want is to follow His recommendations for perfect love of Him. So leave the faceless pack of tepid human beings behind and follow the program that's going to make you sensationally pleasing to God. It's the program that incidentally will also make you poor, completely obedient to Church superiors, and generally sex-starved. This might sound a little rugged, but think about it: How else is God going to know you care if you aren't willing to do crazy shit like this?

It is a hardy band that can do what is necessary to be "religious." It is priests, brothers, and nuns who have taken the three Evangelical Counsels, the three vows that form the cornerstone of the perfect religious life: Voluntary Poverty, Perfect Obedience, and Perpetual Chastity (though wet dreams get a pass). Their vows consecrate them to Our Blessed Lord and they thus belong to Him, to the point that He is willing to overlook the terrible neuroses the vows often create in them.

The rest, the ordinary people, those who choose to slide by in life on a bare-bones program of adherence to the Ten Commandments and the laws of the Church, are called "secular." Before we go on, though, let's be clear on one thing. Comparing the secular life to the religious life is not a matter of comparing a "bad" lifestyle to a "good" one; it is more a matter of comparing a "good" lifestyle (secular) to a "better" one (religious). No one is suggesting that average, avaricious, arrogant seculars cannot live lives acceptable to Our Lord—even if those lives are spent in rich tract homes, fornicating at will to produce potentially satanic, godless spawn, eating in restaurants and depending on their own prideful minds to make menu choices. What we *are* saying is that "better" is clearly the higher calling of the Evangelical Counsels, through which one can live closer to the Lord while never having to file an income tax return or decide what to do on Saturday night, not to mention being able to avoid the mortifying scene at the drugstore when buying condoms. (Note: there may be some exceptions to this last point).

Exercises

1) Why do priests and nuns not get married? Write a turgid report incorporating the notion that nuns are already happily married to Christ, though He *is* on the road a lot. Expand on the fact that even a theoretical marital relationship for nuns would mean finding men (or women, for that matter) who don't mind having their privates whacked with a ruler from time to time. Then explain the core issue that eliminates marriage

for priests, i.e., even if you have a real Papal Bull in your pants, why buy the cow if you can visit the Petting Zoo and handle the calves for free?

2) Religious take a vow to obey their superiors because (a) they themselves have been wrong about everything so far; (b) their moms aren't around; (c) certain kinds of obedience are a turn-on; (d) obeying their inferiors is humiliating.

3) Following the three Evangelical Counsels is the perfect way to (a) experience psychotherapy; (b) impress your friends; (c) land a good steady teaching job; (d) get a big valium prescription with lots of refills.

LESSON 12

THE FIRST COMMANDMENT OF GOD

"I am the Lord thy God, and the last thing
I expect is a raft of shit from the likes of
you." (Transl., New Revised Manga Bible)

To Help Get You Through This Lesson

This Commandment is all about giving to God alone the supreme worship He believes is due Him. Which includes using capital letters for a pile of otherwise crappy, boring personal pronouns.

But are we right to throw adoration around like this? Is He really so great? Is He *worth* it? How does He stack up next to other self-proclaimed deities like Steve Jobs, Michael Jackson, or Jimmy Kimmel?

Answer? Think about it: None of these other gods has a huge backstory that was first published at the time of the dinosaurs and has been on the New York Times best seller list for over 350,000 weeks. Their names do not as yet appear on any denomination of American currency, and nobody prays to them in the middle of an earthquake. Case closed.

In this lesson, you will be forced to memorize the fourteen chief sins against the First Commandment, i.e., acts that directly impact God's self-esteem. Being a little young yet, you'll have to wait a few years before test-driving most of them, but this is the list (not necessarily in the order of appearance): infidelity, apostasy, belching the alphabet, heresy, owning shoes with lights on them, early onset puberty, not giving a shit, taking part in worship that is not Catholic, presumption, hedge fund management, despair, hatred of God, hatred of your cable company, Mensa membership, envy, predictability, elegance, superstition, self-publishing, sacrilege, and, lastly, going back to count these sins to see if there are indeed actually fourteen.

Now: we are not going to insult you by dishing out the usual palaver about just keeping your head down, praying a lot and insisting you don't really worship Pixar or your iPhone. We know what you're made of. To cover yourself for this Commandment, it certainly can't hurt to frequently say the Acts of Faith, Hope, and Misogyny, adding serious volumes of adoration on top of that, but we can tell you frankly this is not what will get you a starring role in the celestial revue.

What *will* make it all work for you is an old dating technique—Playing Hard To Get. This strategy is right out of the playbook of the Prodigal Son, and is a sure winner. It goes like this: 1) Play it wild and loose for awhile, worshipping anything you like. Ben and Jerry's Chewy Chocolate Obscenity, Dolce and Gabbana birth-control devices, Beyonce's boobs—anything. 2) When you feel God's wrath and frustration building, put it all on hold for a day or two. Feel that tension! 3) After one more magnificent, depraved onslaught—say, getting drunk and singing the Turtles' "Happy Together" while doing blow from Rosie O'Donnell's navel, and broadcasting it all on the Times Square Jumbotron—you have a complete breakdown, weeping and apologizing to God for being such a dissipated specimen of near-humanity. 4) You're home free! In one stroke, you're forgiven by God for your idolatry and are set up as a marquee attraction among the faithful, a success story God will want to use to promote His particular monotheistic agenda. Great job! With your new-found fame, a strong income stream from product endorsements, and a locked-in promise of salvation, you're going to find all that worshipping a whole lot easier to do.

How do we worship God?
We worship God by acts of faith, hope, and misogyny, and through other creative acts of physical, mental, and emotional groveling.

What does faith oblige us to do?
Faith obliges us: first, not to be so totally attached to "rationality" and "reason" and all of that. Sometimes notions that sound completely mad are not 100 percent lunatic;

second, to believe firmly in various wacked-out concepts, once church officials have made encouraging noises about them;

and third, to be willing to defend the very looniest of these notions with a straight face, in public, exhibiting the kind of courage that need not rely on crutches like "evidence," "experience," or "sanity."

What does hope oblige us to do?
Hope obliges us to trust firmly in the advertising claims of good American companies, and in God's promise of Heaven for us, though we be fools and jerk-offs with no claim to anything beyond a few minutes on You Tube.

What does misogyny oblige us to do?
Misogyny obliges us to recognize the obvious primacy of the phallus, and to show the most dedicated contempt for women. Men are correct to be smug, since they are mindful that God has given them and only them a special penal code to live by, but also gifts similar to His own traits, i.e., virility, upper-body strength, and a huge *schlong*, which

confers dominion over 24-hour fitness gyms as well as over most bodyguard and bouncer jobs. Women must accept living in the outer darkness of perceptiveness and emotional wisdom, while acknowledging the fantastic abs and inside basketball moves of men.

Why do Catholics sin against faith by taking part in non-Catholic worship?

Who knows why they do it? You would think Catholics would know better. But they seem to keep coming back to shocking pagan rituals like meditations on peace, or hatha yoga to relax the muscles and focus the consciousness. Some go so far as to attend various typical Protestant rites such as roasting and eating human infants or taking part in sexual orgies with farm animals.

Exercises

1) Asking God to help us pass our exams even though we refuse to study is a sin of: (a) schizophrenia; (b) desperation; (c) academic suicide; (d) nagging.

2) To deny that Christ is present in the Holy Eucharist is: (a) to take away all the zazz from those insipid little wafers; (b) a conversation starter; (c) pretty ballsy; (d) generally done when drunk.

3) Edeltraud carries a "rabbit's foot" in her purse, and has a "lucky horseshoe" over her door at home. She claims these things keep her from being unlucky or getting hurt. Explain how these are different from the scapular medal she wears around her neck or the holy water she slings around her room every night the way a vampire-fearing person uses garlic juice. If your explanation

sounds convincing to you and a couple of your friends, please send it to:

The National Conference of Catholic Bishops
A Super Expensive Part of Town
Washington, D. C. 20007

4) Be prepared to recite from memory the words the Burning Bush spoke to Moses on Mount Sinai, an eternal reminder of Yahweh's masculine power and His covenant with Men—words reprised so magnificently by Steve Winwood (with the Spencer Davis Group) in A.D. 1967:

I'm a man
Yes I am
And I can't help but love you so.

Be prepared to quote Christ when he echoed this same sentiment during one of His team-building weekends with His disciples at His bungalow on the South Shore of the Sea of Galilee. "Blessed are the Men," He said, "for most of them are not women."

LESSON 13

THE SECOND COMMANDMENT OF GOD

"Thou shalt not say anything using God's
or the saints' names *in vain*—thou hast to
really mean it."

To Help Get You Through This Lesson

Frankly, this is kind of a limp Commandment. Most violations won't get you any more afterlife punishment than an extra ten or fifteen minutes in Purgatory—the equivalent of being dropped into a wide-mouth toaster at a light-to-medium setting. Or, say, the time it takes to go through a fiery car wash tunnel. Hence the reason the Second Commandment is now identified by most biblical scholars as the first of a pair of Wimpy Commandments. In both, you'll note that the more stern and strident the pronouncements become, the more they sound like the helium-enhanced voice of an impassioned politician. Or maybe flamenco ukulele.

The heart of this Commandment is never to dishonor God with a casual curse. If you're going to do it, do it right. You do not want to do it **in vain**, without force or effect. Put some *feeling* into it. Mean it. God might not be pleased with your cursing, swearing, or your meaningless or false oaths, but He will respect you as he notes your sinful activity and puts you on the "Likely Damned" list.

What are we commanded by the Second Commandment?

By the Second Commandment we are commanded always to speak with reverence of God, the saints, and holy things, and to avoid using crude language unless for dramatic effect, emphasis, or because we are surprised, in pain, or just very pissed off.

What is an oath?

An oath is calling on God to witness to the truth of what we say. It's not done seriously anymore, because historically God has made a depressingly unreliable witness, and simply cannot be counted on to testify in crucial situations.

What great sin does a person commit who deliberately calls on God to bear witness to a lie?

A person who deliberately calls on God to bear witness to a lie commits the very grievous sin of stupidity. If God can't ever be coaxed to witness to truth, why in hell would He violate His own system of conduct by witnessing to a lie? Come on, wake up.

Is it a sin to take God's name in vain?

Jesus H. Christ! Do we have to spell out the most obvious, stupid-ass things? Of *course* it's a God-damned sin to take God's name in vain.

What is cursing?

Cursing is the calling down of some evil on a person, place, or thing. The seriousness of the sin is in inverse proportion to how truly shitty and useless are the people, places, or things in question. There are some few recorded cases in which cursing a bonafide, raging asshole has actually bestowed grace on the curser.

Exercises

1) Swearing is necessary when: (a) no one believes you; (b) trust fails; (c) your butt is on the line; (d) you say anything about Congress.

2) To tell a lie after taking an oath is a sin of: (a) inconsistency; (b) remorse; (c) sagacity; (d) modest proportions; (e) Catholic bishops.

3) Discuss: What is the difference between cursing and swearing? Do not use illustrative examples, and do not say "Not much, especially if you're really pissed off."

4) Apollonios stood in court under oath and testified that angel food cake was better than devil's food cake. What terrible sin against the Second Commandment did he commit? In Catholic tradition, what do the dessert fathers have to say about what he did? Did Apollonios have his taste buds removed for personal reasons?

LESSON 14

THE THIRD COMMANDMENT OF GOD

> "Remember thou keep holy, happy,
> healthy—and safe—the Lord's day."
> (Transl., *Mother Hubbard's Big Golden
> Book of Religious Law*)

To Help Get You Through This Lesson

The second in the di-umvirate of so-called Wimpy Commandments, this one is all about what the Church wants you to do, or *not* to do, on Sunday, the Lord's day. But before we get into a lot of depressing "Do this" and "Don't do that," we would like to point out the obvious: The glass is 6/7ths full! If Sunday is singled out as the Lord's day, that clearly means the other six days of the week *are not*. With the exception of periods containing major Church feast days, an astonishing 85.7143 percent of every week is wide open for whatever berserk, degenerate behavior you decide to cook up, as long as you make it right later on. (See Part III, the Sacraments and Prayer: Penance.)

First, you're going to need to know why Sunday has been singled out as holy. Believe it or not, one of Sunday's biggest selling points is that *it isn't Saturday*. Saturday was the day of rest for the Jews when their religion was the One True Faith, but after Jesus came along and filed papers with district and local authorities to found His

Church, stipulating clearly that it would be the New One True Faith, He needed to find some hook, a special *éclat*, that unique something to set His religion apart. It fell to His disciples and their progeny to settle on Sunday as the day of rest, providing a vital tool in breaking the fledgling Church out of the pack. They marshaled a host of compelling reasons. They argued that Sunday was, after all, the day of the week when Christ rose from the dead. It was the day the Holy Spirit descended on the Apostles. It was also the day when metered parking was often free in urban areas and restaurants traditionally offered special brunch menus. Most telling was the fact that, through broadcast and cable media, Sunday offered fans the largest ever nonstop, dawn-to-dusk array of sporting events—professional or amateur, violent or boring. It even included World Federation Wrestling, which is of course all of the above.

In today's world, only three things are required of Catholics on Sunday. First, they must assist at Mass. It is permissible for those who are seriously hung over to bring an airsickness bag with them, but they must attend. (Hint: it's best to skip Holy Communion in this situation.) Second, they must hold a subscription to receive a print copy of any Sunday edition newspaper that is at least the size of a small schnauzer.

The third requirement defines what activities are permitted on the Sabbath. Historically, Jewish law set the gold standard in this department, rendering it illegal, or *gefilte*, for Orthodox believers to heat up a Pop Tart, smoke a cigar, shave their backs, or do their nails—much less listen to some Barbra Streisand. By contrast, the Catholic Church, mindful of the needs of modern families, has since 1993 relaxed its standards for Pious Sloth (*stagnatus sanctus*) vis-à-vis those of the strict Seventh Day Judaics. Church law now allows for consumption of food on Sunday as well as one hour of shopping (no use of coupons). It further permits one hour of watching the National Geographic Channel, though any use of the remote is forbidden. What the Church does *not* allow is any work task that can be performed on a day other than Sunday, such as mowing the lawn or having sex with your spouse.

What are we commanded by the Third Commandment?

By the Third Commandment we are commanded to worship God in a special manner on Sunday, the "Lord's day." Nothing kinky, no ritual sacrifice, no wife-swapping or beer pong; God is just looking for a little respect, and for the satisfaction of watching his creatures be materially inconvenienced.

How does the Church command us to worship God on Sunday?

The Church commands us to worship God on Sunday by using a high-handed, condescending, irritatingly paternalistic tone—pretty much the way it commands us to do everything else.

What is forbidden by the Third Commandment of God?

Let's just say it's a long list, including everything from posting bail to choking chickens. The prohibitive cost of self-publishing in bulk and the woeful attention spans of students oblige us to say nothing more specific than that **servile work**, work of the body rather than of the mind, is *verboten* on Sunday. Staying in bed is acceptable, as is looking out the window. And looking for loose change behind the sofa cushions. The rule of thumb is: if you're uncertain—don't.

When is servile work allowed on Sunday?

Servile work is allowed on Sunday when the honor of God or the need of a neighbor requires it. It is also allowed if you can work up a justification for it that you can present to a family member with a straight face. Be aware that this can often take up more of your Sunday than the actual work you were going to do.

Exercises

1) Prepare a three-minute report for your class on the question: Is cooking on Sunday servile work or is it permissible? In your report, tell whether driving over to pick up the Bottomless Bucket of Loaves and Crispy Fish Fillets at Burger King of Kings resembles servile work more than opening a can of Sloppy Saint Joes and nuking it to perfection.

2) Shopping on Sunday should not be (a) sweaty; (b) sexual; (c) homosexual; (d) label-conscious.

3) Going to the movies on Sunday is a sin if (a) you are there just for the soft porn montage; (b) you are seeing a James Cameron film; (c) you're too stoned to follow the story; (d) you put your cell phone in your lap and set it to "Vibrate Sensuously."

LESSON 15

THE FOURTH COMMANDMENT OF GOD

"Honor thy father, thy mother, and anybody
who looks important."

To Help Get You Through This Lesson

Ever wonder why public school children usually play more
physical, orthopedically-oriented games like "Red Rover"
and "Kick the Kid" while Catholic school students are daily forced to spend hours playing "Mother May I"? Or why
until 1962 Catholic schools required choke-chains on all
students through grade four, at which time the Second
Vatican Council gave schools the option of using standard
collar-and-chain leashes? The answer is deceptively difficult: These rules emerged originally from a study of
school discipline presented in the spring of 1913 by an
elitist group of Catholic professors at the American Academy of Junk Science in Porcine, Wisconsin. The title of
the study was, "Shut Up and Sit Down: It's All About Obedience," and its recommendations quickly became the
standard for the American Catholic school, as well as for
the leather-boxing-shorts-and-riding-crop crowd.

The theory has a solid basis in the Fourth Commandment, which requires us to respect and obey *not only our parents, but also a daunting array of lawful superiors.* Insistence on this deference was intended to create
a level of trepidation in children which, to quote the re-

port, "will assure in them—and in future adults—the greatest timidity and circumspection in smelling the butts of other dogs, if you know what we mean."

The study's authors acknowledge their debt to the military "boot camp" model, in which trainers break down the recruits before building them back up. The Catholic school template is exactly the same, minus the "building-back-up" part.

Remember also that obedience to superiors in this lesson also means we are obliged to love our country and to respect and obey its laws and officials in even their most sinister activities, with the proviso that they maintain a consistent, credible scrim of hypocrisy.

The chief sins against the Fourth Commandment are pouting, tantrums, moving the ladder when your dad is on the roof, not wearing your flag lapel pin, and euthanasia.

What are we commanded by the Fourth Commandment?

By the Fourth Commandment we are commanded to respect and love our parents, and to do so freely and without coercion. Giving love on demand might seem like a difficult task at first, but always remember: They said movies-on-demand would never happen, either.

We are also commanded to *obey* our parents in everything, even if those things might be tasteless and unethical, as long as they are not out-and-out sinful.

Does the Fourth Commandment oblige us to respect and to obey others besides our parents?

Besides our parents, the Fourth Commandment obliges us to respect and obey all our lawful superiors, except those who seem especially interested in our wallets or in the waistbands of our underwear. This latter group includes lawful superiors who "creep us out," which on average constitutes 70 to 80 percent of the lawful superior population.

How does a citizen show love for, and a sincere interest in, his country's welfare?

A citizen shows a sincere love for, and interest in, his country's welfare by voting honestly and without prejudice or knowledge of the issues, by paying taxes from time to time, and by killing the citizens of other countries when appropriate.

Why must we respect and obey the lawful authority of our country?

We must respect and obey the lawful authority of our country because it comes from God, the source of all authority. Also because should we choose not to, we risk being picked up in an unmarked car and taken to an isolated location where we will be forced to listen to extraordinary renditions of Judas Priest's greatest hits while being beaten between the shoulder blades with big branches.

What are the chief duties of those who hold public office?

The chief duties of those who hold public office are those activities that will *keep* them in office. And, of course, promoting the general welfare of the person in the restroom stall next to them.

Exercises

1) The Fourth Commandment obliges us to obey: (a) our internet service provider; (b) the Dow Jones Big Ouija Board; (c) that person next to you who smells so good; (d) guys in fatigues who love paint ball.

2) What makes obedience hard is our love of: (a) nachos at 3 a.m.; (b) seeing scandalized adults practically peeing in their pants; (c) art, science, and culture; (d) conscience.

3) Ellspeth was arrested for breaking the law. She admitted she was guilty, but when the judge sentenced her to prison, she said, "Law or no law, the state has no right to keep me in jail, eating off of a partitioned metal tray and using a toilet without a seat." Tell what protections the Fourth Commandment affords the court as Ellspeth prepares her lawsuits against the judge, the bailiff, the court reporter, Marriott's "Envoy Access" prison food service, and Kohler plumbing fixtures. Does she have any grounds for suing her parents? Her lawyer?

What does the Fourth Commandment say about a possible insanity plea?

4) Prosthenius's mother told him to wash the floor. He refused. She spat at him. He shredded her copy of the latest "O" magazine. She poured a pint of buttermilk on his laptop. He microwaved her parakeet. When the police arrived, what section of the Fourth Commandment did they cite in arresting both of them?

LESSON 16

THE FIFTH COMMANDMENT OF GOD

"Thou shalt not kill nor harm thyself or thy neighbor, though thou might occasionally have to put the hurt on other races and/or people who live far away from thee."

To Help You Get Through This Lesson

When Saint Addlebert brought kickboxing to East Anglia in A.D. 971, the local populace was bound to ask, Is kicking ass really Christian? For months after, Church scholars fought among themselves with unprecedented violence in order to resolve the question once and for all. Finally, when the last quill wounds were healed, they had their answer:

Damn straight it is.

That result turned out to be deeply satisfying to both sides, since those who advocated Jesus Christ's famous "turn the other cheek" had been given a perfect opportunity to do just that, and violence was ever after part of the canon of Church law. From world wars to barroom brawls (the other guy threw the first punch), the knuckle sandwich became a mainstay on the menu of the Catholic moral cafeteria. As Saint Paul notes in Curmudgeons (4: 788–793), "Though you have faith that moves mountains, without a left hook you are but a prissy, tinkling cymbal."

However, just because you haven't killed or assaulted anyone, you shouldn't assume you're beyond the reach of the Fifth Commandment. It also requires that we take *proper care of our own spiritual and bodily well-being, and that of our neighbor.* This gets complicated.

Consider the case of Bernard of Clairvaux, the renowned abbot, orator, and patron saint of weapons dealers. To this day, controversy swirls around him and the shocking human damage he wrought in his wealthy, prosperous chain of upscale monasteries. As the inventor of such decadent treats as *foie gras* ice cream, he was accused of providing so well for his monks that he initiated the first documented obesity epidemic, and in doing so committed serious sins against the Mighty Fifth's stern insistence that we avoid inflicting physical injury on anyone—even with overgenerous portions of delectable foodstuffs.

Luckily, now that Weight Watchers is such a large part of international law enforcement in so many countries worldwide, and modern western society now enjoys so many healthy, plentiful, inexpensive food-like substances, this problem is virtually a thing of the past.

What are we commanded by the Fifth Commandment?

By the Fifth Commandment we are commanded to restrain our naturally violent natures and be nice. We are further required to take a walk occasionally, read a good book, and keep at least a few Healthy Choice frozen entrées on hand in the freezer.

What does the Fifth Commandment forbid?

The Fifth Commandment forbids murder and suicide, as well as fighting, anger, hatred, irritation, pet peeves, and pissiness. Also included are revenge, getting a buzz on, and excessive gourmet cooking.

Is self-hatred a sin against the Fifth Commandment?

Self-hatred is of course a sin against the Fifth Commandment, you putrid sack of repulsive genetic material! We emphasize, however, it is a sin only when you have enough common sense left to go to confession and tell a priest about your problem. Otherwise, in expressing your self-loathing without confession you become *so* worthless and detestable you're not actually sinning anymore— you're just telling the truth about yourself.

Exercises

1) Saint John the Apostle said that he who has hatred in his heart for his brother is: (a) preemptive; (b) someone who needs a hug; (c) a guy who is sick of hand-me-down underwear.

2) Crispin found a stick of dynamite and kept it hidden in his house, where he and others might get hurt. He thought, "Now I have a little piece of Nobel's secret for huge explosions and the best libido control anywhere. Can't wait to try it!" Name the ways in which Crispin is dangerously unhinged, and explain which two Commandments he breaks. Tell which end of the dynamite stick is best to open up and stick your tongue into, for a little taste.

3) Road rage, forbidden by the Fifth Commandment, is punishable by death in some pagan countries. Explain how the Christian sections of the United States are superior to these infidel nations for having limited the punishment for tailgating or flipping off another driver to sentences of 10 to 20 years in comedy traffic school, without possibility of parole.

LESSON 17

THE SIXTH COMMANDMENT OF GOD

"Thou shalt not commit adultery, except with thy husband or wife."

To Help Get You Through This Lesson

We realize it is not appropriate to choose favorites among the Commandments, since the New Revised Catechlysm rightly views all the Commandments as its children. That said, we just love the Sixth. After so many centuries, it continues to provide the world with some of the most entertaining and appalling sins, while keeping our tongue-clucking skills in peak form.

Students should know that the Earth was nearly deprived of the Sixth Commandment's charms when, in A.D. 1728, as the Enlightenment raged across Europe, the forces of scientific anarchy attempted to expunge the Sixth from the master list of Commandments, based on the discovery of Restless Penis Syndrome, which at the time claimed to explain all sexual dalliance as purely mechanical phenomena, not subject to normal laws of genuine human recklessness, weakness, and shame. Lucky for us they failed spectacularly, and today we are blessed with all the depravity you could wish for, and with a Sixth Commandment as vital as it is frequently ignored.

The Sixth Commandment requires you to know that you must remain pure and that your body is a Temple of the Holy Spirit. Even if its architecture might not be the best, and though it might smell decidedly rank on occasion, you need to keep your temple blamelessly clean and modest at all times—particularly the spires of the boys and the crypts of the girls.

God and His Church insist that you safeguard your chastity by avoiding all unnecessary dangers to it. For centuries this meant hiding under your bed or insisting that a relative lock you in a closet for long stretches, but in today's modern world it is permissible to walk along the street, shop in stores, and eat food in public establishments, as long as you do so in the winter months when everyone is decently clad. You may even take showers on occasion, if you are wearing proper bathing attire and are appropriately chaperoned. It is a fact that God wants you to enjoy your sensuality, as long as things don't actually get sensual.

What does the Sixth Commandment forbid?

Just about everything. That is, if you're talking about words, looks, and actions, whether alone or with others, that are considered "fun" in today's world. Flirting and squirting, bumping and pumping, bleating and eating, screaming and dreaming, sporking and torquing, licking and wicking—all of it, out of bounds. If you think about, speak about, or engage in, any of these acts of immodesty and impurity, you risk being forced by your local bishop to wear the big scarlet "6" on your chest for up to ten days.

What are the chief dangers to the virtue of chastity?

The chief dangers to the virtue of chastity are: living in a human body, changing your underwear, pole dancing, meeting with a stock broker, peep shows, using the restroom, eye contact, eating anything with your fingers, crossing your legs, uncrossing your legs, smiling, and indecent movies (this includes any film featuring Adam Sandler).

What are the chief means of preserving the virtue of chastity?

The chief means of preserving the virtue of chastity are: just saying no, self-deception, and achieving a comatose state. Also helpful are: praying on your knees (though this position can itself be fraught with danger); going to Mass, as long as you're not going in order to find a sex partner; and having a special devotion to the Blessed Virgin, which includes being full of praise and adoration and not asking her too many personal questions.

Why are there no withering remarks about priests and pedophilia in this section, where they rightly belong?

There are no withering remarks about priests and pedophilia in this section because some things are so distinctly unfunny that even the New Revised Catechlysm doesn't have the sack to address them directly.

Exercises

1) One way to preserve purity is through a special devotion to (a) Clorox; (b) valium; (c) sodium nitrite; (d) castration; (e) taxidermy.

2) Any girl who always "hangs out" with boys is in danger of: (a) wanting to use a urinal; (b) getting hauled in for indecent exposure; (c) gaining experience; (d) being outed as transgendered.

3) We must always be on our guard against dangers to purity because: (a) once you marry, your spouse will be very persuasive; (b) 911 operators do not respond to

purity emergencies anymore; (c) paranoia is real; (d) repairing purity is time-consuming and expensive.

4) Why should we show respect for the human body? (In your answer include references to the market value of healthy, freshly-harvested organs, and the current fee schedules of cosmetic surgeons. Be sure to include data on the stepped-down value of women's bodies vis-à-vis men's.)

5) Eliphaz knows that he ought to say prayers in order that he might keep free from a sinful habit he has, but he neglects to do so. When he offers the excuse that he "has his hands full," should he be condemned for stupid and inappropriate humor, for being embarrassed about specifying the nature of his sinful habit, or for having hairy palms?

LESSON 18

THE SEVENTH COMMANDMENT OF GOD

"Normally, thou shalt not steal."

To Help Get You Through This Lesson

Saint Charles Borromeo, the great international cost accountant, once told Charlie Rose in an interview: "Never touch your capital." Had he been more familiar with the Ten Commandments, he would have known that God had already taken this issue one step further by insisting through the Seventh Commandment that we not touch *anyone else's* capital, either.

This radical notion was fleshed out in Saint Paul's Epistle to the White Collar Crimeans, in which we find the three most modern applications of the Seventh Commandment. First and foremost, we must **respect what belongs to others**. As Jamie Dimon of J. P. Morgan Chase has shown vis-à-vis the assets of the American public, in rare cases it is possible to have so much respect for what belongs to others that you just can't help wanting to acquire it for your very own. Nothing could be more laudable, especially considering the historical precedent set by princes and prelates from Pepin the Embezzler to Pope Brigandous XI. Second, we must **live up to our business agreements**, especially if no remedies are available to afford us a comfortable degree of legal protection. Third, we must **pay our just debts**. Whether it's the strenuous efforts of the Iraqi government to find all those forklift pallets of hundred-dollar bills that seem to have disappeared in 2003 and 2004, or the heartwarming story of Angelo Mozilo repaying all customer losses incurred through Countrywide Financial Corporation by donating the proceeds from the sale of his bestseller *Pimp My Mortgage*, we are surrounded by fine examples of this aspect of the Seventh Commandment.

What is the Seventh Commandment of God?
The Seventh Commandment of God is: Normally, thou shalt not steal.

Why do we say, "Normally"?
We say "Normally" because states without active consumer fraud statutes offer truly irresistible opportunities, and because some individuals, through no fault of their own, have heavier cash requirements than others, e.g., expensive house and boat payments, and thus must employ whatever options are available to make ends meet. As it states so memorably in the Old Testament, "Shove it up their Holy of Holies."

What does the Seventh Commandment forbid?
Besides most forms of stealing, the Seventh Commandment forbids cheating too much, keeping what belongs to others unless we're absolutely sure they won't care, unjust damage to the property of any entity other than the Federal Government, and the acceptance of bribes by public officials who do not have a Political Action Committee or another legally recognized money-laundering operation.

Are we obliged to repair damage unjustly done to the property of others?

Of course not. We don't know where *you* live, but just the graffiti and minor vandalism performed each week in most parishes would break most people. At a stretch, you might be considered your brother's keeper, but in no way are you the keeper of your brother's windows, exterior paint jobs, or lighting fixtures.

Exercises

1) If we have a stolen article in our possession, we must: (a) file off the serial number; (b) be thankful for what God provides; (c) make sure to wipe it clean of finger-prints; (d) gloat.

2) We have to respect the property of others because: (a) our own stuff is so crappy; (b) respecting property is always easier than respecting people; (c) worshipping it would be idolatry; (d) the League of Women Voters recommends it.

3) Melchior is a policeman. Lothario said to him, "I'll give you a dollar if you look the other way while I steal from this donut shop." Melchior became upset, pulled his service revolver and tried to shove it up Lothario's left nostril. "A dollar!" he exclaimed. "Do I look like a charity to you?" To calm his nerves, Melchior ate a dozen old-fashioned glazed while Lothario cleaned out the register. Tell why Melchior didn't collect his dollar, and whether their little arrangement should be considered part of both of their pensions. Are old-fashioned glazed donuts a tax deduction?

LESSON 19

THE EIGHTH COMMANDMENT OF GOD

> "Thou shalt not bear false witness against
> thy neighbor, though evasive or confusing
> witnessing is acceptable."

To Help Get You Through This Lesson

We have all heard that famous bibulous quote: "Ye shall know the Truth, and the Truth shall increase a thousand-fold the circulation of the tabloids." If you're like us, you always thought this was just another jewel of wisdom with no application whatsoever to the world—like practically everything else in the Bible. But its relevance to the modern interpretation of the Eighth Commandment is significant.

Traditionally, the Eighth is telling us **not to spread lies, detraction, slander, or calumny** about anyone. Not for sport, not for spite or revenge. Obviously the correct call. That approach gets you nowhere. Instead, you should be taking cues from publications like the Globe and the Enquirer, and, if you feel compelled to speak or write about someone, first get your hands on *truths* that are far juicier than some flight of fancy you could concoct in a moment of vengeful feeling or general distaste. All you need is a good camera with a telephoto lens, maybe some sensitive recording equipment, and a little *chutzpah* (ancient Hebrew, meaning "leadership, initiative, and courage"), and in no time you're actually making money selling these truths to publishers, or at least back to their originators for safekeeping. For fun, you can even just put the information up on the internet.

Remember, the Eighth is telling you not to pole vault to conclusions and injure the good name or honor of another person through falsehood or snap judgment. But it is only common sense to use the truth to best advantage. Get into the game!

What are we commanded by the Eighth Commandment?

By the Eighth Commandment we are commanded to speak the truth in all things, even if the truth can be had only after a long, laborious stakeout, too many visits to Jack in the Box, and fouling the car interior and camera equipment with bacon grease and secret sauce. The good name and honor of others is always paramount, since it makes the scandals more shocking, and thus more lucrative.

When do people commit the sin of rash judgment?

Usually when they're in a hurry, or have done a lot of uppers. Or if they really need to pee and there's no bathroom nearby. Also if they are drunk, it's late, and the person they just met is pretty cute.

When do people commit the sin of detraction?

Generally, when people lack enough verifiably true information to properly massacre an entire reputation, they will resort to using untruths to nibble around the edges, which is the sin of detraction. A pity really, and so unnecessary. It is the result of simple laziness.

When are we obliged to keep a secret?
We are obliged to keep a secret until someone is crazy enough to tell us one.

Exercises

1) To believe something evil of another on a slight suspicion is: (a) intuitive; (b) engrossing; (c) Lutheran; (d) eventually borne out.

2) To make known another's sins without necessity is the sin of: (a) standup comedy; (b) political campaigning; (c) biographers; (d) the priesthood.

3) A priest once told Ambrosina to take a bag full of feathers and throw them off the roof in a high wind. She did so, standing downwind, and choked uncontrollably for several minutes. Then the priest told her to gather up every one of the feathers. She said, "That's impossible!" "Exactly, my child," he said. "And so it is in trying to repair the harm done by detraction and calumny. So what must be done?" the priest asked. Ambrosina suggested going to Target and getting a couple of standard, medium-soft fiberfills for $9.99 each. Was Ambrosina correct in going with hypoallergenic material? Was she getting the best deal?

LESSON 20

THE NINTH AND TENTH

COMMANDMENTS OF GOD

"Thou shalt not covet thy neighbor's wife in any perceptible way."

"Thou shalt not covet thy neighbor's goods, but rather obtain thine own through creative use of credit."

To Help Get You Through This Lesson

To bring you into the picture here, "coveting" means desiring or wanting in a way that's over-the-top, like Cookie Monster facing a big bag of hash brownies. Explaining this whole thing to you is honestly kind of embarrassing for members of the clergy, often because they themselves are doing some serious coveting even as they explain. In any case, we are not going spend lots of time on these Commandments, because at your age it's natural that your coveting skills will be pretty crappy, even if ours aren't.

Whenever you finally get the hang of it, though, these are the go-to Commandments for painfully over-scrupulous and repressed young Catholics to find their preferred brand of self-condemnation. If you've always been an armchair warrior, if the idea of performing actual sins in the physical world seems "icky" to you, then these

Commandments are your thing. The no-muss, no-fuss alternatives to actual adultery, stealing, and any number of other jugular vein violations of God's law. This is what Saint Donald of Barthelme used to refer to as "locating myself in the abstract, where I am always more comfortable." That is, rather than actually stealing candy from a store, or playing strip poker with the kids next door, you have only to *think* about these things in order to qualify as a serious sinner, ready to confess your transgressions.

There is a catch, of course.

In each case, you have to *enjoy* the thought about the sin before it can be bonafide and confessable. If it's just a quick flash of a thought, one that you don't "entertain," it is classified only as "temptation." Don't let this discourage you: Once you get started, even the attempt to distinguish between what is temptation and what is actually sinful can be just as exciting and diverting as sinning in the real world. So don't give up on these!

What are we commanded by the Ninth Commandment?

By the Ninth Commandment we are required to be pure in thought and desire.

The editors must here refrain from describing what might, at your young age, make you impure in your thought and desire, since to do so would automatically make you impure in thought and desire.

When do thoughts about impure things become sinful?

If they're among those that theologians call "really juicy," then thoughts about impure things pretty much become sinful right away, because we deliberately take pleasure in them. J. C. Penny's Sunday supplement of swimsuit ads, for example, is bound to make instant, horribly debased sinners out of the best of us. Avoiding temptation is the only way out of this—so cancel that newspaper subscription. (And don't look at the ads on smart phones or electronic tablet formats either.)

What are we commanded by the Tenth Commandment?

By the Tenth Commandment we are required to muster at least minimal, lukewarm sincerity—with no tinge of envy—in admiring the material wealth amassed by our neighbors. This includes even the most tasteless and offensive displays of consumer greed, so common to many of our neighbors.

What does the Tenth Commandment forbid?

The Tenth Commandment forbids all desire to stare at, stroke, drool on, take, or keep unjustly any deeply materialistic items belonging to those who have been seduced by such dross. Tellingly, the Tenth does *not* expressly forbid obtaining any of these same items by running up a credit debt so large that you and your family are forced to clothe yourselves in Glad lawn and garden bags, and to eat domestic pets for sustenance.

Exercises

1) The best remedy against desiring your neighbor's wife is: (a) moving to a neighborhood of hideous people; (b) desiring her husband instead; (c) remaining roughly nine years old; (d) getting to know her.

2) Possession of too many material things is harmful to: (a) closet space; (b) your bank balance; (c) delusional modesty; (d) Hey, define "too many."

3) Daydreaming, like idleness, is the devil's workshop—and the craftsmanship is often superb. P. T. Barnum, winner of the 1946 Nobel Prize for Marketing, one day realized he was thinking hot thoughts about the ample bosom of the Three-Breasted Woman, a member of his latest exhibit. He quickly said a fervent "Hail Mary," and then made himself busy doing something. Only a few minutes later, he had invented the "blister pack," which would win him another Nobel. When do bad thoughts become lucrative, and not just sinful?

PART III

THE SACRAMENTS AND PRAYER

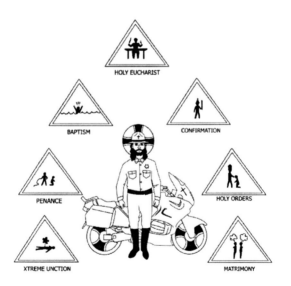

" TO PROTECT, TO SERVE AND TO JUDGE "

LESSON 21

BAPTISM

"Unless a man be born again of water, spirits, some ice and lime zest, he cannot enter the kingdom of God. There is the possible alternative option of watching thirty-five to forty hours of Deepak Chopra videos, but that would likely send you back to the first option anyway." —John Bradshaw, Ch 3, Verse 5

To Get You Through This Lesson

When you came down the chute and blasted out of your mom's insides like a daredevil performer out of a circus cannon, you cried like, well, a baby. You knew instinctively you had already offended God and everyone else in the Catholic community by being clad only in "Original Sin," also known as the "Sin of Adam," at your debut. This is actually more than one sin, since Adam and his registered domestic partner Eve offended God not only by fornicating with monkeys, but also by associating with a known criminal, vandalizing a tree, and engaging in public nudity. Slowly you learn that you were indeed born a reprehensible shithead, and that you bear some responsibility for hip-hop music, Steven Seagal movies, and the mess the world has become.

But then there was the good news: Baptism.

Okay, so after Adam's gross failures you'll never have beatific visions or preternatural powers on Earth or anything, but Baptism does promise that you can get the monkey off your back and have a slim chance of surviving the wrath of a God who would dump you into a seething cauldron of hellfire on a whim.

That's because when you do get baptized, Original Sin is *washed away*, leaving you cleansed and smelling like Febreze, ready to grow up and commit your own personal sins, which must be dealt with differently. (See sections on Penance and Confession, or see the Scorsese film *The Departed*.)

Important to remember: There are people living in the world who do not have access to the Truth. They don't know about the crucial nature of Baptism, or about any of the sacraments. The good-hearted among them are often dangerously adrift in life, with no direction other than trying to find a cure for AIDS or cancer, or to alleviate hunger in developing countries. Sad, yes. Sad to contemplate that for lack of a splash of water and ten or fifteen words, these decent barbarian souls will never see Heaven.

But wait. Now there's a solution, and it's not necessarily whatever liquid you've been using in performing Baptisms. No, it's a set of special dispensations for these pure souls, ones that, through *symbolic* Baptism, cover entry and all attractions in Heaven *without water or a ceremony or even any awareness of the vital role of Baptism.*

Sound too good to be true? Well, it *is* true. And here are the four ways the noble heathen can achieve the salvation promised by Baptism without ever feeling the shock of cold water:

a) Baptism of Desire. This is achieved when a person loves God above all things, without really knowing Him, and desires to do all that is necessary for his salvation, though he doesn't really know what that means, either.

b) Baptism of Blood. This applies to those who suffer martyrdom for the faith of Christ while remaining blessedly free of any specific notions about it.

c) Baptism of Pathos. This is the crucial approach for people who are so utterly helpless, confused, and miserable that God gets a little exasperated, but ends up feeling sorry for them. Finally He says: Great, terrific, okay, let's just get on with it. So you're baptized, all right? Now clear off.

d) Baptism of Broadway. This is exclusively for truly great stage performers, those who can do it all: sing, dance, and act. God admires these triple-threat, blockbuster performers so much that they are automatically baptized when He believes they've passed the threshold of transcendent excellence in performing. One of the great jokes in this category is that Sammy Davis, Jr. believed he had converted to Judaism, but in the latter part of his life—surprise!—he was actually a baptized Catholic.

What is Baptism?

Baptism is the sacrament that gives our souls the new life of sanctifying grace by which we become children of God and heirs of Heaven. This is a great deal, no question. Whether you are a grown-up having an infant baptized without his or her consent, or someone just waking up to the potential value of the inheritance, it's hard to pass up something as sweet as this. You are just one short ceremony, one splash of water away from getting a piece of the action in the only Unreal Estate that matters: Heaven. Though there is no stated market value attached to any of this, and appraisal data is sketchy, if God's name is associated with it you know it's a solid deal.

Can anything other than water be used to baptize?

The answer is yes . . . but it's complicated. There have been periods of history in which liquids other than water were more standard in the baptismal ceremony, and the method of baptism also was quite different—more enthusiastic and copious than the one currently practiced, strangely resembling what we today would call "waterboarding." For example, during the Great European Drought (1240–1884), priests and monks routinely used wine or even brandy in generous baptisms of the faithful, their families, and even of themselves if they felt the need for a little "booster."

Today, a small volume of water on the forehead typically defines the procedure, though in an emergency it is permissible to use soft drinks, especially Coke, Diet Sprite, and Dr. Pepper. Energy drinks are considered a good choice, though some feel that superstition about their value has crept into the ceremony. Pepsi is naturally forbidden in all baptisms, since it is known to be the Devil's drink.

Who can baptize?

Priests and bishops have dibs, though anyone can do it in an emergency. Say, for example, someone at the party has passed out and appears not to be breathing, and you know they're good people even though they were doing nasty things in the back bedroom a little earlier. The Church says, "Save a soul. Go for it. But not with that rum and Coke—use club soda."

Why is the name of a saint given in Baptism?

The name of a saint is given in Baptism because the name of a cartoon character would be undignified. How could children live with names like "Daffy Duck" and "Olive Oyl"?

Why is Baptism necessary for the salvation of all men?

Baptism is necessary for the salvation of all men because it is "the gateway to the other six sacraments," and without it you can't get married, die a proper death, or ever hope to be assigned the "Parishioner of the Month" parking space at church. More importantly, if Baptism were not necessary, then this section of the Catechlysm would be far too short to justify the dollars the reader has forked over. (Note: If you did not pay for your copy, please review Lesson 18: The Seventh Commandment of God.)

Exercises

1) Rebecca was studying hard to become a Catholic, for she wanted to save her soul as Christ commanded. One day while swimming she drowned without having been baptized. What chance has she for salvation? Would you say "none," since she was a selfish little twerp interested only in saving her own pathetic little soul? Or would you finesse it by pointing out that her drowning was a form of Baptism after all? Or would you invoke the solemn Ecclesiastical Gimme that in effect says, "Hey, close enough"?

2) Evangeline is going to have her two-week old baby baptized. She told the priest that she wants her brother, a Catholic who has never gone to Mass and has not made his "Easter duty" in years, to be the godfather. After

the priest advised her brother to use a reliable, over-the-counter laxative if it had been that long since he has made his Easter duty, what advice did the priest give Evangeline? Other than to discover the identity of the father of the baby, buy him a decent suit, and get him to the Baptism?

LESSON 22

CONFIRMATION

"And they were all filled with the Holy Ghost—or another brand-name intoxicant of equal or greater value—and began to speak with other tongues, as the Spirit gave them utterance." —Acts, Ch 2, verse 4

To Get You Through This Lesson

Okay. So the story is that in Confirmation, the Holy Ghost comes to you in a special way. We are clearly not talking about courier services, handheld electronic devices, or sexual positions here, but more about what the Holy Ghost, through the Church, can do to strengthen the faith and resolve of eleven- or twelve-year-olds to make them perfect Christians and soldiers of Jesus Christ. This, at a time when children's bodies are experiencing hair growth in awkward places, and when they are becoming enormously inventive in their recreation.

Confirmation is usually administered by a bishop, whose job it is to stop all that.

In other words, Confirmation is a symbolic coming-of-age ceremony meant to ensure that you never, under any circumstances, actually come of age. It's like a Vision Quest without the hassle of the Vision. Or the Quest. Like a bar mitzvah without the Torah or the big platter of chicken liver spread.

Major point: Don't let the ceremony be intimidating. Unless you do something crazy or original, you know you will end up with lots of sanctifying grace, a blast of a special sacramental grace not available in stores, and a unique imprint on your soul, much like a tattoo, but one that doesn't lower your IQ by 40 points and destroy every job interview you'll do a few years later.

Because the bishop will want to know that you, as a soldier of Christ, are well-versed in the chief truths and duties of your religion, you will have to answer a question or two, usually from the Catechlysm. No big pressure. What you say can be incomplete or even a little incoherent, since the bishop is obliged to be in a good mood and leave no one out of the ceremony. As long as your answers don't have him looking at you like you have something hanging out of your nose, you are pretty much in.

What does the bishop do when he gives Confirmation?

The bishop extends his hands over those who are to be confirmed, in a gesture meant to celebrate Charlton Heston's classic poses in *The Ten Commandments*, and to recognize some of the great backup singers of the '80s. He then prays that those before him may receive the Holy Ghost without being thrown to the floor by a mighty wind or having their hair catch fire. An audible gasp will come from the congregation as he lays one hand on the silken curls of each finely formed young head, and with the other anoints their forehead with holy chrism in the form of a cross. A kind of blobby cross, true, but still a cross. He's finger painting, after all. Give him a break.

What is holy chrism?

Holy chrism is a mixture of olive oil and balm, blessed by the bishop on Holy Thursday, under a full moon, with a steel band playing "I've Got You Under My Skin." If you get any of this stuff on your good clothes, by the way, you'll end up having your butt confirmed by your father's holy leather belt.

Check our web site for some delicious free recipes for using your holy chrism. It's absolutely miraculous as part of a spiritually balanced breakfast, lunch, or dinner!

What is meant by anointing the forehead with chrism in the form of a cross?

By anointing the forehead with chrism in the form of a (blobby) cross is meant that the Catholic who is confirmed must always be ready to profess his faith openly, and to submit fearlessly to the most obscure and embarrassing rituals that the Church can dish out, including having grease smeared on your forehead.

Why does the bishop give the person he confirms a slight blow on the cheek?

First, to be clear, we are talking here about the cheeks located on both sides of the nose and mouth, and not what the English call the "bum," the French call "*fesses*," and what Americans call the politicians they don't like, using any number of vulgar synonyms.

So the bishop administers to the person a slight blow or tap on that facial cheek to remind him that he must be ready to suffer everything, even death, for the sake of Christ. Very much like losing five dollars on the Lotto can be a stark, chilling reminder of what it's like to be destitute. The bishops have wisely elected not to advocate inflicting symbolic pain by pulling out the razor-sharp bowie knife, called the "Christ Avenger," which they all keep under their robes, and plunging it into the midsection of each person being confirmed. It was agreed at the Council of Baton Rouge, in A.D. 1124, that this would lead not only to unwanted prosecutions, but to substantially smaller congregations.

What are the effects of Confirmation?

The effects of Confirmation are: an increase in sanctifying grace, a special sacramental grace, mortifying grace, get-out-of-jail-free grace, certain social graces, and a boxed set of seasons one through three of *Will and Grace*. Side effects may include bowie knife lacerations, greasy forehead, and chrism poisoning.

Exercises

1) The most powerful weapon of a soldier of Christ is: (a) strong situational ethics; (b) a 40-gallon margarita fountain; (c) a good set of radial tires; (d) a good set of foregone conclusions; (e) a sense of irony.

2) List the Catholic radio and TV programs in your area, being sure to include "So You Think You Know Shame and Guilt," "The Catholic Needlepoint Hour," and "Who Wants to Be a Hypocrite?" Write a letter to thank your local station for having the dedication to broadcast these revenue sinkholes. Watch all the shows for several months, then write about the suffering this caused you. (Do not be afraid to embellish: If you want proof that God loves a good bullshitter, you need look no further than the Irish.) Was it the 3 or 4 a.m. time slots that were hardest? Or the heart-stoppingly boring topics? The smarmy host or hostess? Express yourself as much as your repression will allow.

LESSON 23

THE HOLY EUCHARIST

"My ready-to-eat goodness is already baked into this bread that has come down from Heaven." —John of the Hostess cakes, Ch 6, verse 41

To Get You Through This Lesson

As usual, we're going to bring it down to you right from Heaven: You're *never* going to understand this lesson. Hell, *we* don't understand it. And that's the point: This sacrament is a mystery. A mystery wrapped in a piping hot dogma, usually served with poorly made wine. But since we've hacked through all the historical and ecclesiastical underbrush, we can give you the bottom line.

In the Holy Eucharist, three things happen: Christ's body and blood, soul and divinity, blood pressure issues and credit history—all of it—are contained under the appearances of bread and wine; then they are offered to God as a sacrifice; and then are received by you in what is called Holy Communion. This last bit means you are going to eat Him.

Obviously, this is hard to swallow. The most childish person knows that the molecular weight of bread is different from that of human flesh, even when adjusted for inflation. So how does Christ pull this off? As we will see, He does it by doing what He does best: being powerful. All-powerful, in fact. First, He uses what is called in Latin His *Transubstantio Mojo*, which allows him to change the substance of bread and wine into His own actual body and blood. (Amazing He can survive a blood alcohol of 13.5 percent—easily high enough to kill anyone else. It makes Him a walking taxable event with the federal regulatory people, too!) As if that weren't enough, when the bread and wine become HIM, He then uses His Don't-Scare-The-Children powers to *maintain* the appearance of bread and wine. If He did not take this miraculous second step, after the transformation (called the Consecration) you would immediately see Christ Himself and not bread as your intended meal, which would bring up, if not your breakfast, at least very serious issues about cannibalism as well as about bacterial contamination, cooking temperatures, and so on.

If this seems too wacky to be taken seriously and is starting to make your Mormon friends look saner, you should know that the dispute about whether the bread and wine actually do *become* God's body and blood is very crucial. It has caused hundreds of thousands of people to hack one another to death over the past, say, thousand years, and—almost as impressive—has generated millions of pages of writing that are every bit as impenetrable as a Sony owner's manual.

You need to know that the pilot project for this daring excursion into metaphysical haute-cuisine is called the Last Supper, a meal Christ shared with His twelve Apostles the night before He died, during which He first called on them to eat His body and drink His blood. It is not recorded whether anyone present had the *cajones* to refuse, though since it was the end of the meal it would have been reasonable to beg off on the grounds of being "completely stuffed." You also will need to remember that Christ gave the Apostles the power to perform this rite over and over. When He said the words, "Do this in memory of Me," He thereby created a priesthood as well as a huge industrial sector for bread and wine production (known in the media today as Big Bread and Big Wine) which continues today, having survived product recalls, soggy crusts, union scandals, political corruption, and the invention of Thunderbird and Hot Pockets.

What is the Holy Eucharist?
The Holy Eucharist is like a small albino potato chip that is perfectly round and flat. It comes only in "original" style; there are no jalapeno, nacho cheese, or cool ranch flavors, nor is there a "crinkle-cut" variety. The Eucharist should never be contemplated as a partner for sour cream and onion dip, in any case. No, the Eucharist is served à la carte, one per customer (no coupons), to the faithful during Mass. In the Holy Eucharist, under the appearances of bread and wine, the Lord Christ is contained, offered, and received.

When did Christ institute the Holy Eucharist?
The only existing press releases, ultimately incorporated into the New Testament, tell us that Christ instituted the Holy Eucharist at the Last Supper, the night before He died.

Who were present when Our Lord instituted the Holy Eucharist?
When Our Lord instituted the Holy Eucharist the Apostles were present, along with two roadmen, a couple of handlers, the caterer, and the publicist who first came up with the idea of using the word "instituted" to drive home the point that the organizational Church and this idea of the

Eucharist were going to be *big*, and last thousands of years.

How did Christ institute the Holy Eucharist?
It is not clear exactly how Christ instituted the Holy Eucharist, because all the legal paperwork (trademarks, patents, notary work, caterer's invoice) was destroyed when Jerusalem's city hall was burned to the ground by enthusiastic fans after a big soccer victory over Egypt in 1356. From traditional sources like the New Testament, we do know he said something to his Apostles along the lines of "Take some bread and eat it; this is My body." Then, taking a cup of wine, He blessed it, and said, "This is My blood of the new covenant which is being shed for you guys and for many others for the forgiveness of sins. But please don't take this as a huge guilt thing."

What is transubstantiation?
A transubstantiation is a natural cave that is made into a connecting subway stop. How did this question get in here?

Did anything of the bread and wine remain after their substance had been changed into Our Lord's body and blood?
After the substance of the bread and wine had been changed into Our Lord's body and blood, there remained only the appearances of bread and wine. But having the appearances is a great break for us. Without them, the bread and wine would lose visibility, which could make partaking in the sacrament difficult. You could mime eating the bread and drinking the wine, but somebody would be sure to call you on this "emperor's-new-clothes" approach to the Eucharist.

Add to that the fact that whatever actual nutrition the bread and wine contains rests completely in the appearances, and the whole thing is a win-win!

Does this change of bread and wine into the body and blood of Christ continue to be made in the Church?

You bet it does. It is a free market issue, essentially. A century or so after Christ, demand went through the roof, and you can imagine the mad scramble to bring supply into line with demand. Brick-and-mortar churches, priests, bread, wine—it was bullish all the way around. Though not so robust now, the market is still solid.

Why does Christ give us His own body and blood in the Holy Eucharist?

Christ gives us His own body and blood in the Holy Eucharist:

First, because to give them to us in a TV dinner or a corndog would be blasphemous.

Second, so that he would be acceptable to the discriminating church member who insists on both substance *and* appearances.

Third, because it is much more efficient and cost-effective than obliging Christ to re-incarnate every generation or so and having to undergo the whole ministry, death, and resurrection saga again and again.

Exercises

1) All who receive the Eucharist are one body in Christ because the bread is: (a) cheap; (b) carnivorous; (c) an equal opportunity snack; (d) psychedelic.

2) If you put a host under a microscope you would see: (a) God's enlarged pores; (b) a huge dark blob, probably the tip of your finger; (c) the error of your ways; (d) an impressive array of tiny quilts made for Christ by Clara Barton; (d) narrowly targeted product placements.

3) After Piotr, a non-Catholic, visited a Catholic church, he said to his Catholic friend Ishmael: "I saw a red lamp burning before the altar; people who came in and went out bent their right knee to the floor, everybody kept their eyes looking almost all the time at the high table with decorations behind it and nobody was talking. What is the reason for all these things?" Ishmael answered, "Piotr, you tool! You went into the bondage parlor next door to the church! Those people were waiting for Taskmistress Myra the Avenger to come out and perform her Table-Top Backdoor Humiliation Ritual. Good thing you left—it costs eighty bucks!" What more could Ishmael have told Piotr about Myra's clientele?

LESSON 24

PENANCE

"Whose sins thou shalt forgive, they are forgiven, and whose sins thou decideth to leave in place, they shall stay in place until the poor bugger in question rots from the inside and is carried away by drooling winged beasts to the deepest chasms of Hell. And havest thou a nice day." —Book of Sartre, Ch 1, verse 666

To Get You Through This Lesson

True, Penance can seem a little scary at first. But because it is so important a tool in shaping your long-term strategy for saving your soul, you've got to dig deep, belt up, grow a pair, and whatever other shallow, crappy expressions you use to motivate yourself. Remember that Penance is the *only* sacrament by which *all your sins* committed after Baptism can be forgiven through **absolution** by the priest. Not to worry: "absolution" does not involve bathing or showering with the priest. Absolution is a "washing away" of your sins, an extraordinary and solemn power Christ Himself gave only to his Apostles and to the millions of their painstakingly selected successors who have dished out the forgiveness over the centuries.

And now they're going to dish it out to you.

Can't wait? Well, to make it an optimum experience for all, and for the magic to work properly, there are a couple of things to keep in mind before diving in. First, you need to be **sincerely sorry** for your sins. Not that kind of earnest, angst-ridden, furrowed brow stuff you see on so many faces in the pews, but *real* sincerity. The kind that's so good even you yourself can't tell if you're sincere or not. You've got to climb down into the tiny crevices of your intentions and ruthlessly root out any breath of artifice. Strip yourself naked, rip the very flesh from your bones if there is even the barest chance that a single grain of inauthenticity might be lodged there, just out of your view. Practice in front of a mirror if necessary.

Second, you are going to need to confess all of what you find to the priest in the **fullness of Truth**. After all, the priest is taking on the daunting task of acting as teacher, judge, referee, coach, chaperone, sponsor, midwife, warden, bagman, buddy, and doctor of souls, and the least you can do—considering all the trouble he has gone to, and how hard you have worked at being sincere—is to offer him the unvarnished Truth, from the tenderest, most easily bruised parts of your heart and psyche, being totally vulnerable to him by telling him all the grimy details of the evil you've done. He's not going to hurt you.

What could go wrong?

What is the sacrament of Penance?

Penance is the sacrament by which sins committed after Baptism are forgiven through the absolution of the priest, without any airtight agreement on your part to refrain from committing the same sins again. You are in effect giving up your right to remain silent about your sins, but getting a big concession in return. Everybody wins.

Whence has the priest the power to forgive sins, and to use the word whence?

We must all lay off the word *whence*. How is the Church going to retain its venerable profile if it can't use a de-lightfully antiquated word hither and thither?

The priest has the power to forgive sins from Jesus Christ, who said to the Apostles and to their successors in the priesthood: "It's thumbs up or thumbs down on these wankers, boys. It's going to be your call." (Note: For greater clarity, this quote was subject to judicious modifi-cation of vocabulary and syntax while scrupulously main-taining the "feel" of the original text.)

With what words does the priest forgive sins?

The priest forgives sins with pretty much whatever words he feels like using, usually in Latin so you won't know what they mean anyway. For priests in America, popular song lyrics have been big recently—Billy Joel, Queen, and Sinatra very often—along with the more traditional Broadway show tune lyrics.

What are the effects of the sacrament of Penance, worthily received?

The effects of the sacrament of Penance, worthily received are:

First, the restoration or increase of sanctifying grace (actual increases may vary, check your soul's fanny pack before and after receiving the sacrament);

Second, the forgiveness of sins, including the ones you couldn't remember, as long as you actually couldn't remember them, in which case you would not be aware of this special benefit, so forget it;

Third, suddenly becoming a very competent yodeler;

Fourth, help to avoid sin in the future—but not, like, *too much* help. You will be a lot like a water-resistant watch in a full bathtub;

Fifth, a powerful case of the munchies.

What else does the sacrament of Penance do for us?

The sacrament of Penance also gives us a greater appreciation of other world religions, none of which apparently requires over-the-top shit like Penance.

Exercises

1) A non-Catholic said to Perpetua: "I believe that God alone can forgive sins. I cannot believe that a priest, who is a man like ourselves, can do so." If you were Perpetua, why would you tell this non-Catholic that he is a vacuous little twit who reeks of the most degrading possible Protestantism espoused by Martin Luther, a man who had a gaggle of horse-faced apostate nuns for a harem and who never bathed?

2) Thinking over our past sins is called: (a) reminiscing; (b) hot fudge for the mind; (c) fantasizing; (d) algebra class; (e) foreplay.

3) In giving absolution, the priest: (a) asks detailed questions; (b) scrubs your back with a loofah; (c) makes you beg for it; (d) perspires heavily.

LESSON 25

CONFESSION

"Unless you repent, you will all perish."

—Luke, Ch 13, verse 3

To Get You Through This Lesson

We realize this quote from Luke sounds like a flat-out threat, but you have to remember that Luke was a physician. Doctors just don't have people skills. Think of reading Luke as part of your personal Penance.

He does make a good point, though: In a head-to-head comparison, repenting sounds a lot better than perishing. So what can we do to totally dominate the repentance game? How can we ace the ritual of confession, first time, every time?

Number one, smart confessing is always about the highest quality kind of sorrow for sins (or "contrition," as the pros call it). It's called *perfect* contrition, and you get it by being sure that you are sorry for your screw-ups because you really love God and feel bad about offending Him. You can do this even if God hasn't friended you on Facebook, isn't on your speed-dial, and has never arranged to have His face appear to you on a piece of toast. You can love Him even if you don't know Him—if you're not sure about His sense of humor, His politics, or His personal hygiene—because He is the Savior of the World.

As a class of beings, Saviors of the World are uniformly pretty good. So your obvious move is to love a good guy. How hard can it be?

Your second option for contrition when you confess is called *imperfect* contrition, and it's for derelicts, weirdos, barmies, artists, underachievers, and people who never wear a tie. Which is to say: it's not for you.

Imperfect contrition exists when you are sorry for your sins because you are afraid the Lord will drop you into Hell like a stone because of them. You're sorry all right, but it's a pathetic kind of whiney regret that God despises, frankly. You may get into Heaven, but you'll be in the bleacher seats—the sticky ones, where somebody spilled a large Coke.

A good example of these two contritions: You've taken the low road when you admit you robbed that Chase Bank near your home and are now sorry because you got caught. That's *so* imperfect. You should be saying that the real reason you're sorry is your powerful love for the executives of Chase, and the fact that the robbery was offensive and hurtful to them. *That's* perfect contrition.

There is a little-known third option for contrition, too, but because it is just this side of Hell it is rarely referred to. Catechlysm Insiders and veteran aficionados of regret know that it exists basically to make the Imperfect Contrition crowd feel better about itself. It is called Malcontrition, and is the default position for people who are so disoriented by Penance that they have lost all will to falsify their behavior. This severe condition prevents the soul from taking any nourishment, as well as denying it all automobile club discounts and forbidding it to rent furniture of any kind. For those interested in a graphic picture of the effects of Malcontrition, see the 1955 classic Robert Ikea film, *Dead Men Can't Eat*, starring Burl Ives and Lana Turner. Look for Meister Eckhart, who puts in a brilliant cameo as a fresh fruit tart.

Number two, you can't qualify as a real Confessionator until you've mastered the topic of punishment. Without this crucial ingredient, Confession would be humane, merciful, and altogether unrecognizable.

Unfortunately, Confession isn't the Inquisition, so all the truly creative physical punishments so painstakingly devised hundreds of years ago by Dominic de Guzman, patron saint of secret police and intelligence agencies, are not in play here. The modern Church spells out only two broad categories of punishment that they demand: eternal and temporal.

Do not sweat either one of these. The "eternal" punishment is not very eternal. Without your lifting a finger, it vaporizes when you confess all the most terrible of your sins—the Mortal Sins—such as murder, armed robbery, and masturbation. Temporal punishment is, not altogether logically, a little harder to get rid of. Beyond the magic of the priest's absolution, to get rid of temporal punishment you actually have to perform some activities that will cause you pain, like going to Mass, fasting, reading the daily news, or watching World Federation Wrestling. You'll catch on; because if you don't, you risk losing your immortal soul.

(Just messing with you—relax and memorize some answers!)

What is Confession?
Confession is the opportunity to talk to an authorized priest (be sure to ask to see ID) about all the disgusting things you have done, so he can absolve you of the bad juju you created and prescribe suitable punishment while creating in you a rich inner life of shame. All at absolutely no cost to you!

Why must we confess our sins to a priest?

We must confess our sins to a priest because not to do so would deprive him of a nice little income stream. All priests in the USA operate with a special dispensation to change the names in the sinful situations they hear about in Confession, and sell the stories to Garrison Keillor, Fox News, or *Hustler* Magazine.

Is it necessary to confess every sin?

No, just your own. You're not even old enough to know about the ugliest ones, so for now slow down and stick with "I disobeyed my mother twice."

What are the chief qualities of a good confession?

The chief qualities of a good confession are five: It must be humble, sincere, entire, plausible, and convincing. It should have brisk pacing, a decent plot line, and some French words in it—with proper pronunciation, too. If you are not careful, being boring in Confession will earn you another mortal sin.

What happens if we knowingly conceal a mortal sin in Confession?

As Saint Augustine said nearly a hundred years ago in a famous beer commercial, Go For The Gusto. By that Augie meant if you have really embarrassing mortal sins to confess, it's best to go to Confession drunk, so you don't remember any of them. Being severely impaired in memory, speech, and vision lets you off the hook for concealing sins, if not for raiding your parents' liquor cupboard. You're in great company, too, since being unable to remember anything is a powerful defense used successfully by public figures from Pope Pius XII to Ronald Reagan.

You can make it work for you, too! (Note: If you are planning on going to Confession sober and concealing a mortal sin, be sure you have chosen a great place to hide it, because God will be really pissed if He finds out.)

Why does the priest give us a penance after Confession?

The priest gives us a penance after Confession not just to help us make it up to God, who can be kind of sullen and churlish even a week after you've been forgiven, but also because research has proven a good penance helps us avoid 15-20 percent of most sins in the future. (Please note that the statistical effective range is reduced to 4–6 percent if sins involving sex and/or money are included.)

Why does God require temporal punishment for sin?

God requires temporal punishment for sin to teach us the great evil of sin, though He admits a good instructional video would probably more easily achieve that goal. He also requires it to satisfy His lightly vengeful and sadistic side, and to warn us not to sin again. Or at least to allow a decent interval.

Where do we pay the debt of our temporal punishment?

If you're thinking MasterCard or Discover, you're really not paying attention. We pay the debt of our temporal punishment either in Purgatory, suffering heat nearly as intense as that of Hell or Palm Springs in July; or in this life, being obliged every time we are driving on the freeway to stay behind an older lady in a Buick Regal, who can barely see over the steering wheel and who never does more than 40 mph.

Exercises

1) Christ wants us to admit our sins to a priest in order to destroy our: (a) digestion; (b) reputation; (c) fun; (d) reliance on drinking games for catharsis.

2) To heal all the effects of sin, God must send us: (a) sex toys; (b) a whole lot more than He's sending right now if The Bastard really expects true healing; (c) to Heaven for a getaway weekend; (d) brand name pharmaceuticals at a fraction of retail prices; (e) more durable beliefs.

3) Since our cross to bear is everything God allows to happen each day that we do not like, or each thing He wants us to do that we don't like, or in many cases just His overbearing and annoying presence, each student should make up a list of crosses that come up in his or her life. Any mention of the New Revised Catechlysm in this list will be dealt with severely.

   If after making your list you feel your crosses are not heavy and difficult enough for your taste, then you are ready for the creative act called Customized Mortification; that is, creating your own painful crosses to maximize your suffering, which does away with all that punishment in Purgatory that involves so much suffering. If you get where we are going with this. Here are a few suggestions to get your creative suffering juices flowing:

   a) When you are eating that grape popsicle on the playground at lunchtime, instead of finishing it, sacrifice the last half by dropping it down the front of your shirt or blouse. There's suffering galore here. It's wickedly cold to start with, and horribly sticky later. Extra bonus suffering: your clothes will be permanently stained and your mother will be inspired to think of even better ways to cause you suffering.

b) When you finish brushing your dog, collect all the hair, clip it into small bits and drop them into your underwear. It will be a prickly, chafing, rash-inflamed day for you—just chock full of the most satisfying suffering. This is called "hair-skivvies," a modern variation of the medieval favorite called the "hair shirt," which has been appreciated for centuries by saints and simple masochists alike.

Enjoy! Or rather—don't!

LESSON 26

XTREME UNCTION

"Even though our outer man is decaying, our inner man is being renewed in the eternal circle of multiple personalities."
—Second Corinthians, Ch 61, verse $x + y$

To Get You Through This Lesson

Here is a sacrament that is just now, in the last three or four centuries, finally coming into its own. After being misunderstood ("What's an Xtreme Munchkin?") and limited to the narrow demographic of dying people, it has at last become a real brand that appeals to young and old alike.

So what is it? In a nutshell, Xtreme Unction is another of those sacraments where the grease hits the forehead. It requires a substance similar to what is used in Confirmation or Holy Orders, but minus the trans fats. That is, instead of a gloppy slug of thick paste (known among good Catholics as the Viscous Circle), a tasteful thread of thin oil is massaged onto the forehead—also behind the ears and between the breasts of the recipient. Caution: this sacrament can only be administered by a priest; anyone else performing the ritual may be subject to sexual assault charges, or to the even less attractive possibility of being groped by a person too incapacitated to do it properly.

It is through a combination of holy oil massage, prayer, and New Age music that the priest provides the sick person with a spiritual goodie bag of valuable premiums better than anything you ever found under your seat at a taping of Oprah's show. These premiums, most of which we can't seem to remember right now, help sick people feel better about being sick, so they are a little less pissed off at God. This, in turn, promotes the Perfect Love of God that is needed to get them into Heaven when they actually do die. It's not enough to have the Near-Perfect Love of, say, Richard Burton and Elizabeth Taylor, or Brad and Angelina, or Siegfried and Roy. The kind of Perfect Love you are required to have for God when you die is rare and hard-won—enough so that it makes sense to build as much practice into your life as possible, before the BBR (Big Body Rot).

As the Church says in its current online advertising: Xtreme Unction! It's not just for death anymore. Boys and girls, why not afford yourself the opportunity to practice your Perfect Love skills until even the thought of Perfect Love makes you nauseous? Why not do it anytime, under the full protection of Holy Mother Church, when, say, you're sunburned or you've skinned your knee? Or when you're dealing with a case of head lice? And tell your parents there are opportunities for them, too, at every level of discomfort: from a simple hangover to a bout of road rage, or an unexpected STD—anytime they're not feeling their best.

Remember, three levels of service are always available through your parish priest: There's the **Pick-Me-Up**, for times when things seem hopeless, your cable service is down, and Domino's isn't answering their damn phone; **Lumps and Bumps**, which includes broken bones, Hepatitis C, and help for young people in dealing with the invisible but noxious household fumes generated by their parents' dysfunctions; and **The Last Gasp**, formerly known as "Outroduction."

What is Xtreme Unction?

Rumors will say it is the dance your drunk uncle does on the picnic table on the Fourth of July, or the brand name of a lube product used on the NASCAR circuit, but the truth lies somewhere in between. Originally designed as spiritual help for those who are breathing-challenged, Xtreme Unction is a chance for all Catholics to score some sanctifying grace (the Dom Perignon of graces), whether you're headed out for a Lady Gaga concert, a 20-day stint on a BP oil rig, or any other near-death experience.

Who should receive Xtreme Unction?

All Catholics who are in danger of death from sickness, accident, or from being born are theoretically eligible, but the pool is severely reduced because those eligible must also have attained the use of reason.

Who can administer Xtreme Unction?

The party line says that only a priest can administer Xtreme Unction, but with the modern interpretation of the sacrament just about anyone with decent motor skills and fantasies about being a cleric can do it. It is especially easy now, with so many boxes located on the walls of restaurants, bars, and other public places. These are clearly marked "Unction Function—Break Stained Glass In Case of Boredom or Emergency." Each contains not only a high-quality, deep-moisturizing oil (SPF 35), but a sturdy cardboard Roman collar for the person performing the sacrament, and the complete lyrics to both "Kumbaya" and "They'll Know We Are Christians By Our Love."

What are the effects of the sacrament of Xtreme Unction?

The effects of the sacrament of Xtreme Unction are:

1) Relief from dry, flaky skin, particularly on the forehead, behind the ears, and between the breasts;

2) The miraculous appearance of Bundt cakes and casseroles on the front porch of the home where the sacrament is performed;

3) A lot of testy questions from close relatives about whether this sacrament is ever really necessary, or perhaps could be done online;

4) The spiritual strength to ask your doctor for a second opinion.

Exercises

1) Xtreme Unction helps us acquire: (a) a good laugh; (b) more colorful and elaborate curses; (c) a tryst with a daytime television star; (d) fragrance-free ecclesiastical products.

2) Xtreme Unction usually: (a) coats and protects the stomach; (b) is pretty depressing; (c) will not kill you; (d) scares the shit out of the sick person; (e) is not tax deductible.

3) Reginald is taking a plane across the Pacific. He feels he will be in great danger on this trip and wants to be anointed before he goes. Why does the priest tell him he is a horribly twisted, neurotic little jerk whose

whole life is explained in the DSM-IV and who should get a spinal transplant?

4) Organize the class to set up a model sick table, simulating Xtreme Unction, with different students bringing in the necessary objects. Think of it as a spiritual scavenger hunt: One brings the candles, another the matches. Someone brings the oil, someone else brings the tofu chunks. When you finally have the scouring pad, the Grey Goose Vodka, the Phillips screwdriver, both jars of strawberry jam, and the fondue pot, see who can arrange everything best on a small nightstand. Anything falls on the floor when it's your turn, you do a shot!

LESSON 27

HOLY ORDERS

"No woman, no cry."
—Book of Marley, Chapter Umpteen, verse deuce

To Get You Through This Lesson

The sacrament of Holy Orders presents us with one of those tantalizing contradictions in Church teachings which at first seems a little ridiculous but only later begins to appear truly insane. In the finest sense, of course. It is this: To become a bishop, priest, or minister of the Church you must have a penis, but you must not use it, other than to remove liquid waste from your body. Even in that act, too much "grasping" and "touching" is not acceptable. A priest knows it is far better to let his waste run on his shoes and the floor than to be tempted to do too much "aiming."

Through Holy Orders, what appears to be a perfectly normal man becomes empowered to perform supernatural acts and to be "another Christ." This should be enough to induce any man or boy to give up plans to become a doctor or a mental patient. Why become someone who *thinks* he is God when you can actually *be* God?

Major theme of this lesson: the priest as mediator, or go-between, whose work is to bring together God and man. Results have been spotty, true, but we must keep in mind that we have been at this for only 2,000 years, so it is way too early to indentify a clear trend.

Though the job of mediator is as hopeless as it is thankless, it does not mean we should be any less respectful to priests, and should always compliment them on whatever richly-embroidered, brightly-colored serape they decide to wear in church on a given day.

Keep in mind that in your overarching strategy to obtain an exclusive mansion in the heavenly housing development, the priest can be the difference between your landing in a majestic, brilliant white granite number with Doric columns, and getting tossed into a rumpled bungalow with yellowed pull-shades and hollow-core doors. He is a key player, like a much-admired real estate broker, whose favor you want to curry and whose eggs you want to coddle (though you do not want him coddling yours). Trying to get into Heaven without the priest's intermediary work is doomed to a failure best illustrated through stories of famous figures from history like Gautama Buddha, Lao Tse, and Gandhi.

So dump all those preconceived notions of priests as nerds and sociopaths who make scrimshaw with the bones of third graders and who use the same handkerchief for months at a time. Whether your plans involve becoming another Christ, or just someone interested in connecting with the people who'll make sure the Celestial Big Dogs remember your name, Holy Orders deserves your attention.

What is Holy Orders?

Holy Orders is the sacrament through which men receive the power, grace, financing, and social standing to perform the sacred duties of bishops, priests, and other ministers of the Church, for the most part without getting caught.

What are some of the requirements that a man may receive Holy Orders worthily?

That a man may receive Holy Orders worthily it is necessary:

First, that he have a pulse;

Second, that he have sexual equipment that surpasseth understanding;

Third, that he spend at least half of his TV time watching Bravo;

Fourth, that his library of porn should be large enough to prevent his ever being tempted elsewhere;

Fifth, that he have a lifetime supply of Tic-Tacs.

What is meant essentially by a vocation to the priesthood?

By a vocation to the priesthood is meant essentially that the still, small voice in a man's head—the one that was suggesting for awhile that he stalk Katie Couric and then that he should preserve all his bodily waste in old mayonnaise jars—is now telling him he looks great in black, has a promising set of gin blossoms, and should apply now to the U.S. Department of Cult and Religious Affairs for the Deluxe Clerical Lifestyle Grant, which includes a choice of male or female housekeeper who, aside from proven cooking skills, knows how to serve it up hot.

What are the effects of ordination to the priesthood?

The effects of ordination to the priesthood are:

First, yet another increase in sanctifying grace, to the point where he begins to wonder if he should donate some for a tax write-off, or destroy some to increase the value of his current holdings;

Second, a sudden affinity for watered silk;

Third, a facial tic, often;
Fourth, a huge party after the ceremony.

What are the chief supernatural powers of the priest?
The chief supernatural powers of the priest are: changing bread and wine into the body and blood of Christ, being able to find his car keys no matter where he lost them, and continuing against all odds to keep women out of the priesthood.

Why should Catholics show reverence and honor to the priest?
It's about knowing where your bread—body of Christ or not—is buttered.

Exercises

1) A candidate for Holy Orders must have the intention of devoting his life to: (a) mastery of contract bridge; (b) becoming a bishop; (c) learning the value of deodorant; (d) a painstaking chronicling of pay-per-view boxing matches.

2) A priest receives his priestly powers from: (a) Rotary International; (b) the estate of J. R. R. Tolkien; (c) an undisclosed breakfast cereal; (d) listening to lots of Johnny Cash albums.

3) Let two or three of the boys be assigned to present to the class a report on "A Day in the Life of a Priest." They could interview one of the parish priests to get the necessary information, so long as the priest is not deliberately and flagrantly honest, and does not use his answers as his recruiting tool, or vice versa.

LESSON 28

MATRIMONY

"What therefore God has joined together, let no man put asunder without first addressing the salient legal questions. And not unless there is, like, a really good reason for it."
—Book of Deceptions, Ch 4, exhibit A

To Get You Through This Lesson

Let's not kid ourselves: Matrimony is about fornication. Fornication and the epic struggle to legalize it. Even before the time of Christ, humans realized fornication was a disgusting and depraved act to which they were inexorably drawn, much as we today are drawn to all-you-can-eat buffets. In many ancient pagan cultures it was taken for granted that you could get a major in Fornication Studies at virtually any underground university, and charter fornication schools were popping up all over the Cradle of Civilization. It was a nightmare of messy hypocritical activity, crying out to become a more acceptable, white-washed hypocrisy. And it fell to Jesus Christ to do something about it.

Keep in mind we are not talking about homosexuality here. If fornication could be compared to legal trade after the establishment of the sacrament of Matrimony, then homosexuality is like smuggling, i.e., bringing the goods into an illegal port of entry.

We are not talking about masturbation, either, since that is a personal agreement entered into between a person and his/her private parts. The level of sinfulness it represents has to be taken in hand on a case by case basis by the priest hearing the perp's confession.

Before Jesus revolutionized the field, marriage was thought of in the most traditional legal terms involving dowries, land rights, Sears gift cards, and the effective enslavement of women. But in A.D. 31, after attending a string of depressing and embarrassing stag parties in Bethesda and Tel Aviv, Jesus had an epiphany that changed all that. (It had been many years since His first epiphany, but they are rare by definition.) He created a new, totally different kind of marriage: one that focused on dowries, land rights, Sears gift cards, and the effective enslavement of women, yes, but this time the agreement was between *two baptized Catholics, who were then free to boink their brains out whenever they felt like it and still be respectable citizens.* This assumed the understanding that they would fornicate only with each other, and that the decision to do it be left to the man, of course.

The rest is history. From that moment, when the rush to respectability began in earnest, we can trace the peaceful, loving evolution of male/female and extended family relations as well as the establishment of the total and enduring peace among all nations that we enjoy today. Oh, wait, no. Sorry. That's our bad. All of that will have to wait for universal health care and the legalization of marijuana. But don't worry—it's all on the way.

What is the sacrament of Matrimony?
Matrimony is the sacrament by which a baptized man and a baptized woman bind each other for life in a lawful mar-

riage—and sometimes to their bed frame in postures of submission—and receive the grace which allows them to discharge their marital duties as well as their bodily fluids.

Why does the bond of the sacrament of Matrimony last until the death of husband or wife?
The bond of the sacrament of Matrimony lasts until the death of husband or wife not just because, as a conservative, God loves stable societies, but because in modern times one of the partners will invariably attempt to murder the other within the first few years.

Why has the Catholic Church alone the right to make laws regulating the marriages of baptized persons?
The Catholic Church alone has the right to make laws regulating the marriages of baptized persons because in the last few years all major hotel chains have laid off their Chaplain/Event Coordinators and ceased offering their attractive Wedding Packages. It also helps that through the centuries the Church has retained much of the charmingly dogmatic and authoritarian character that saw it through the Dark Ages, the Inquisition, and the Thirty Years War.

What authority has the State regarding the marriage of baptized persons?
They don't got squat. As Jesus said, "Render unto Caesar the things that are Caesar's—like zoning complaints, landfill logistics, and bond issues to build professional sports facilities—and render unto God the things that are the most supernatural and cool, and ultimately the most lucrative." (See the section entitled "Collateralizing the Vatican Museum.")

What is necessary to receive the sacrament of Matrimony worthily?

To receive the sacrament of Matrimony worthily it is necessary to be in a state of grace and to obey the marriage laws of the Church. She'll need to pretend to be less intelligent than he, and he will have to be able to get an erection.

What are the chief effects of the sacrament of Matrimony?

The chief effects of the sacrament of Matrimony are:

First, an increase in sanctifying grace and sales of home furnishings;

Second, the man developing a sudden taste for single malt scotch and online poker;

Third, the woman deciding to stop going to the gym.

Exercises

1) Marriage lasts: (a) for what seems like an eternity; (b) as long as you keep licking it; (c) until the Cubs win a World Series; (d) until a disastrous appearance on "The Newlywed Game."

2) The power to dissolve a marriage belongs to: (a) the witness protection program; (b) the TV remote; (c) Angelina Jolie; (d) morning breath like fish emulsion.

3) One day Prospero had to go into a house to stop a quarrel between a husband and a wife. After being threatened with prosecution for trespassing, he said: "I do not know what is the matter with those two Catholics, always fighting!" This lesson teaches us what is the matter. Explain it to Prospero. Why does Prospero call 911 and then start in with a speech about the duties of

the marriage partners to each other before he bothers to find out that this husband and wife are not actually married to *each other*, and that the subject of their constant fighting is which of them has more sanctifying grace. Is Prospero wrong to fix everyone a drink and suggest they sit down and relax?

LESSON 29

THE SACRAMENTALS

"When I was a child I played with childish things, but when my voice changed I had to get a job and put away my sacramentals."
—Some Epistle of Paul: can't find the chapter or verse

To Get You Through This Lesson

Here is another case where the New Revised Catechlysm makes the tough calls no one else wants to make, boys and girls.

Think of the Catholic Church as a house (kind of an old house, with serious maintenance issues, but that's another story) and the sacraments as the various rooms in the house. You know: maybe the bathroom is Baptism, the dining room is the Holy Eucharist, and the basement—that special dank spot where we store all the junk no one ever sees—is Penance. Now, to follow this crappy analogy a little further we could say that Sacramentals are the little closet where the Church keeps her slightly embarrassing, kitschy swag, (or *tchotchkes*, if you want a touch of Old Testament flavor). Open that door and what do you find? According to the party line, you've got "holy actions and things" that are "somewhat" like the sacraments. Just like the guy who rings up your groceries is somewhat like

146

George Clooney except that he's homely and knows nothing about acting. You've got crucifixes, statues, water blessed by a priest, holy cards, devotional candles, scapulars, holy pictures, little glow-in-the-dark plastic figurines of Jesus and Mary. How about a Saint Christopher medal? The guy's not even a saint anymore and you can still get his medal.

You get the idea. These things are fun, sure, and most are available in the parish gift shop for less than $6.99, but, bottom line, they're not very useful in helping you grind out the yardage needed for the heavenly touchdown you're trying to score.

This doesn't mean you can take a pass on memorizing the Q and A, though. What do you think, this is Sesame Street?

What are sacramentals?
Sacramentals are holy things or actions that the church uses to provoke modest outbreaks of piety and shameless requests for favors while dodging the issue of superstition.

How do the sacramentals obtain favors from God?
Sacramentals obtain favors from God through the unbeatable combination of ironclad belief in their power and abject toadying. If these don't get you your favors, you should know anecdotal evidence suggests that threats against God are a poor alternative. If all else fails, you can always try appealing to His mother.

What are the chief benefits obtained by the use of sacramentals?
The chief benefits obtained by the use of sacramentals are:

First, a sweet kind of pathetic optimism;
Second, protection from telemarketers;

Third, assurance of successful future garage sales;
Fourth, new enthusiasm for 99-cent stores.

How should we make use of the sacramentals?

The sacramentals should be used with faith and devotion—as party favors, pet toys, tips in restaurants and clubs, Halloween treats, drink garnishes, aquarium décor, wedding gifts—the sky's the limit. Great as part of a pickup line at your favorite bar, too!

Exercises

1) Sacramentals inspire: (a) pathos; (b) minor twinges of devotion; (c) commercial urges; (d) morticians.

2) Sacramentals were instituted by: (a) latent human madness; (b) holy persons with questionable taste; (c) holy persons with execrable taste; (d) vengeful non-Catholics.

3) It would be a sin against the First Commandment of God to use a sacramental as pagans and Italians use their "lucky pieces" or charms. They cannot *of themselves* help us, unless we are crazy enough to believe they can. Magog foolishly says: "I am not afraid to drive my car at dangerous speeds, because my 6-speaker Bose stereo has been blessed by the bishop, and I have a Saint Christopher medal in my crankcase." Why does Magog make no mention of his air bag system or his new 60-mph "cow catcher" impact bumpers?

LESSON 30

PRAYER

"I chant a little prayer for you."
—Deus Warwick, pop song, verses 1
through 4

To Get You Through This Lesson

Put simply, prayer is the conversation you have with God to convince Him to give you what you want. But we should never put this "simply." There is real art in this high-stakes game of groveling, so before you plunge in, make sure you've got a solid grasp of the fundamentals.

First, a little history. Prayer is as old as Adam when he asked God for a companion, and when, a little later, he asked God if there maybe wasn't another way to make the companionship thing work out for him. Prayer has been used by man to help find food and shelter, to conquer enemies, to win bets, and to get laid. It is also *the* prime tool to help you both get into Heaven and be certain that your local sports franchises are victorious.

Prayer remained primitive until the Himalayanese invented the prayer wheel in the year 84,912 (A.D. 1688) when they moved out of their mountain fastnesses, trekking down to the Mediterranean Sea in search of warmer weather and better dentistry. Though hugely significant, that invention never really took off because of the tribe's refusal to license the hardware. The world of prayer was changed profoundly, however, in 85,035 (A.D. 1811), when the steam-powered prayer wheel was invented by Robert Fulton. This miracle-making machine could grind out ten times as many Lord's Prayers per minute (LPMs) as the old device, and without the loss of so much slave labor to carpal tunnel syndrome.

Astonishingly, only a few short decades later this invention fell prey to competition from the more efficient and less expensive wind-powered prayer flag, created by Betsy Ross in 1852.

Today, modern prayer comes in two flavors, mental and vocal. *Under no circumstances should you confuse the two.* Vocal prayer is most suited to situations in which you are in the presence of like-minded toadies, at which time it is sensible to drone on in unison for a dreary but hopefully profitable hour or two. Mental prayer, by contrast, is a solo activity during which, through various means, you silently attempt to convince God of your worthiness. To make these prayers audible in inappropriate settings such as subways, super markets, locker rooms, or massage parlors is to invite incarceration for madness, or worse, nomination to political office.

So, how to talk to your Creator? Do not tell jokes. Do not try to cajole. God has no sense of humor, which you would know if you read your Bible more frequently. Start by playing to the jealous streak He manifests so often in scripture. That is: do some serious sucking up.

You can most easily remember how to do this by the acronym WTF: **Worship** him (build Him up); **Thank** Him for everything, even if you think He hasn't done much for you lately; and beg him to **Forgive** you for whatever little slights He is imagining you've inflicted on Him. Only then should you make your move. Only then have you earned the right to push your agenda. Only then

can you claim to be truly loaded with prayer, truly full of
it.

What is prayer?
Prayer is the lifting up of our minds and hearts to God,
trying at the same time to avoid thinking about where
they were before we lifted them up.

How should we pray?
We pray:

First, understanding that it's probably best not to be
stoned at the time;

Second, in English, since God always respects English
speakers more than the barbarians;

Third, with some mood music working in the back-
ground, maybe Barry White or Kenny G;

Fourth, having made a pit stop beforehand, since
nothing breaks the mood like announcing in the middle of
your prayer that you have to take a leak.

For whom should we pray?
Your prayers should be for yourself, obviously, but to
make it less crude throw in some family members whose
names you remember, maybe a few movie stars, sports
personalities, and pop singers. Also mention a few people
you hate, since this is impressive proof that you are a
humble and forgiving person—great stuff if you can be
convincing.

Why do we not always obtain what we pray for?
The number one reason you do not obtain what you pray
for is that you are ignoring all the valuable tips provided
by the New Revised Catechlysm. You think we are doing

this for our *health*? Are you memorizing your questions and answers or not? Get with the program.

The other reason you will hear is: God saw that what you asked for would not be for your good. Your answer to that canard is that you're not asking God for His opinion, you're asking Him to give you what you want. Full stop.

Are distractions in our prayers always displeasing to God?

Distractions in our prayers are not always displeasing to God. In fact, if the prayers are idiotic enough, He finds the distractions a positive relief.

May we use our own words in praying to God?

You may not use your own words in praying to God. Making up words from whole cloth will lead only to confusion, leaving God frustrated and unable to understand you. Only snake handlers, government bureaucrats, and the looniest evangelicals would try a stupid stunt like this. Use standard English at all times.

How do we usually begin and end our prayers?

We usually begin and end our prayers with a few calisthenics—stretching, deep knee bends, jumping jacks, that sort of thing. Staying limber is key to a fine prayer life. The real masters of prayer, such as the Desert Fathers who sat praying for days in their caves on the outskirts of Carson City in what was then the Nevada Territory, established rudimentary parcourses for this very purpose, allowing visitors unlimited free use of them.

Why do we make the sign of the cross?

We make the sign of the cross any time of day to express the mystery of the Blessed Trinity and, at the checkout counter, to take advantage of special values on brand names you trust at participating Big Baldacchino Catholic Warehouse Stores. Some restrictions apply.

Exercises

1) In prayer, we must listen to God with our: (a) physical restraints in place; (b) iPods; (c) legendary attention spans; (d) what was this about, again?; (e) fortune-teller's full cooperation.

2) Distractions in prayer are sinful if: (a) someone else is having them; (b) they involve Martha Stewart and/or Johnny Depp; (c) God gets confused by them; (d) law enforcement can trace them back to you.

3) Agrippina found it hard to pray in church because a baby was crying across the aisle from her. But every time she found her mind wandering she brought it back again to her prayers. Would you say her prayers were pleasing to God in spite of the fact that she was praying that the baby would just die right there in church?

APPENDIX

WHY I AM A CATHOLIC

APPENDIX

WHY I AM A CATHOLIC

"Because I've got everything you'll ever need right here." —Mary J. Blige

We all know why we are Catholics.

It's not about the sense of belonging, our swelling with pride when we consider the rich, magnificently tawdry history of the Church we're part of. It's not about the lineage of the popes that remains unbroken through long, colorful periods of creative corruption that would shatter a lesser institution. It's not about the all-star lineup of historical and contemporary personalities that represent the Catholic team (a lineup, by the way, that the Curia is constantly striving to improve through negotiations like those taking place currently with the Church of Scientology to obtain, through a straight trade, both Tom Cruise and George W. Bush in exchange for Caroline Kennedy). It's not even about the stylish school uniforms allowed to children, or the scrumptious Knights of Columbus chicken-and-creamed-vegetable banquets that are ours to enjoy several times a year.

We're Catholics because Catholics are *right*.

And being right about everything—putting ourselves in the company of all those saints whose footprints and handprints adorn the concrete at the entrance to Saint Peter's in Rome—carries with it the burden of helping all the poor heathen bastards who are so tragically, desperately wrong. How can we best do this?

Well, luckily God has given minds to the heathens, minds only slightly inferior to ours, with which to understand the world, to discover sources of bananas and partners who will pick the lice off of them. As hopeless as they are, for some reason God desires that heathens should use their power of reason to come up with the answers He requires. The same ones Alex Trebek would insist on, but in the form of a question. This is possible for them, and for anyone, for the simple reason that in the entire Catholic playbook there isn't one single teaching that is opposed to **right reason**. Well . . . okay, there *is* that quote from Luke 14, verse 26, about hating your mother and father if you would follow Jesus. And possibly the one from Matthew 16, verse 25, about losing your life in order to save it. That one seems a little light on right reason. Oh, and that thing about Africans not being permitted to use condoms to prevent further AIDS infections, that's probably not the firstborn child of right reason, either. But other than those? Solid.

God is willing to prepare the minds of the Unwashed to receive His word, but it can happen only if they are willing to act a little bit Catholic to start with and meet Him three-quarters of the way. They must do four things: *first*, pray for the light of grace to know the truth and accept it; *second*, pray for the light of grace to figure out what that first thing means; *third*, live what passes for good, moral lives without making Catholics look too terrible; *fourth*, put aside all false opinions about the Catholic Church. Make that all the true ones as well, since they're likely to be heavily negative.

The take-home here: This section is to help you as a Catholic to realize that just because the Church didn't much love Galileo and Darwin, it doesn't mean our faith can't be a matter of both faith and reason, if you are not too insistent on, like, *lots* of reason. We also want to reassure non-Catholics that our religion is not nearly as freaky as it looks from just about every conceivable angle.

In reassuring the pagans, by the way, you must go lightly. Getting into long, drawn-out arguments about points of dogma is so retro, so Counter-Reformation—and simply not productive. What you should be doing is demonstrating to them how different, how much kinder and more thoughtful Catholics are than the rest of the world. You need to step up and be a real Christian: compliment their hair or their clothes, laugh at their jokes, offer to give them a foot massage. Show them some of your best dance moves. All of these things represent far more compelling evidence of the truth of Catholicism than any theological discussion. They also might get you laid.

How can we prove that there is a God?
We can prove there is a God because only by the almighty power and wisdom of an eternal and intelligent Being could we be showered with blessings like okra, ice hockey, Demi Moore, cargo pants, and the real clincher—flush toilets.

How can we prove that the human soul is immortal?
We can prove that the human soul is immortal because when our bodies die and decompose, there is no trace of the soul left. It has already flown to Heaven, or south for the winter, or whatever.

How can we prove that all people are obliged to practice religion?
The horrible welts on the backs of the secular slackers should be proof enough.

How can we prove that the only true Church of Christ is the Catholic Church?

We can prove the only true Church of Christ is the Catholic Church mainly because it's really old—maybe not quite so old as the Egyptian dynasties, but older than Maximilian Robespierre or Hugo Chavez. Also, you can tell it's the only true Church because it has the coolest music, the finest graphic arts, and the most outrageous clothing of any group carrying the Christ brand. Perhaps Saint Minimus the Great expressed the authenticity of the Church best. Minimus was bishop of Guam in the late fourteenth century, finally becoming pope shortly after his death in A.D. 1393. "Imitation is what these other churches will be doing, when they finally arrive on the scene," he wrote. "And we all know that imitation is the sincerest form of stealing."

Whence do we chiefly derive our historical knowledge of Jesus Christ, His life and teachings, and of the Church He established?

Most of this historical knowledge comes to us from a series of thirty powerful Bible bubblegum cards, originals of which are hard to find these days. Equally reliable traditional sources have been the backs of cereal boxes, Denny's placemats, various books of the Bible, and some oil paintings in Europe.

Besides being historical records, what else are the books of the Bible?

Aside from being passable historical records, the books of the Bible, taken together, are excellent tools for rodent and insect control. They are also a valuable accessory for low-impact step aerobics, and a serviceable kiddie booster seat for home or restaurant.

Are all the truths revealed to us by God found in the Bible?

Not all the truths revealed to us by God are found in the Bible; some are found in the smooth draw and rich flavor of Marlboro Lights; many are found in the eighteenth Harry Potter book, *Harry Potter and the Secret of the Acolyte's Underwear*; and some are found in those miraculous, rare, ecstatic interludes when everyone has decided to leave you the hell alone for once. Did we mention Divine Tradition, too?

What is meant by Divine Tradition?

By Divine Tradition is meant the summer camp convocation on the Costa Brava that has been held for select Church Fathers every year since A.D. 325, when the Council of Nicaea turned out to be so terribly tedious for many attendees. Divine Tradition is built around a Gregorian karaoke competition, a couple of contract bridge and canasta events, a Frisbee football league, and a terrific nude volleyball tournament, Romans versus Orthodox, held at the end of the three-week event. It is here that, down through the years, the Church's *crème de la croix* concocted so many of the truths taught by Jesus and His Apostles, truths which were given to the Church only by "word of mouth" and not through the Bible.

Why must Divine Tradition be believed as firmly as the Bible?

Divine Tradition must be believed as firmly as the Bible because Church Fathers have worked damn hard over the last eighteen hundred years to supplement a pretty rickety story with many richly inventive gems of doctrine that frequently approach coherence, especially those that were enunciated in the seventh and eighth centuries, during the 3 to 5 p.m. sessions, between water sports at 1:30 and joyous-hour drinks at 5:30. The very least that members of the Church can do is accord them the same respect they routinely show to spin doctors in the secular world.

How can we best show our gratitude to God for making us members of the only true Church of Jesus Christ?
We can best show our gratitude to God for making us members of the only true Church of Jesus Christ in two ways: first, by going out and finding people who are not members of the Church, offering them the chance to join, and persecuting them right there in the street if they refuse; and second, by purchasing huge numbers of Catechlysms to give to friends whose souls you feel might be at risk. We are convinced this will be a large population not just because of the dissolute nature of contemporary society, but also because the editors of the Catechlysm are in serious need of cash infusions, having developed austere but expensive tastes in just about everything.

HEY, PAX VOBISCUM!

The New Revised Catechlysm Guarantee

We unconditionally guarantee your physical, emotional, intellectual, spiritual, and psychic satisfaction with this book. (We can also guarantee the eternal salvation of your immortal soul, if you wish. Please contact us for pricing.) Write to us at:

New Revised Catechlysm
Ascetic Village Manor Estates
Rancho Salmonello, CA 66666

If for any reason you are not 100 percent satisfied with *The New Revised Catechlysm*, we will immediately be impressed by your discriminating taste, and powerfully devoted to you for your willingness to give us money for such a shameless piece of garbage.

163

THE REAL ACKNOWLEDGEMENTS

If we're dishing out the plenary indulgences, first in line is the estimable editor Michael Wilt, whose godly patience and expertise were critical in shepherding a messy flock of words into a shape much more celestially pleasing than any of our monks dared have hoped for in this Vale of Tears. Hearty thanks to Cleofe Pacaña for her creative illustrations and her courage in dealing with sudden outbursts of obsessive-compulsive disorder; and to Brad Norr for brilliant cover art that makes us appear both original and creative, though of course we are merely Catholic.

Lastly, to my old friend and very critical reader Lawrence E. Johnson, Esq., who applied the lash at crucial moments, and who was even willing to employ Catholic guilt techniques to motivate completion of the manuscript. *Et cum spiritu tuo*, you maniac.

NOTES

Yes, on page 48 we are referring to the brilliant, honorary lapsed-Catholic comedy team, The Firesign Theatre. This quote comes from their classic album *Boom dot Bust* (Rhino Records, 1999). Check out "The Devilmaster," demon expulsion machine from Infermco. Visit firesigntheatre.com

And page 99 includes a quote from Donald Barthelme, a genius and actual lapsed Catholic whose postmodern uses of guilt and shame would be awe-inspiring even to a *high-quality* parodist. The quote is from the story "Critique de la Vie Quotidienne" (*Sixty Stories*, Penguin, 1982).

CPSIA information can be obtained at www.ICGtesting.com
Printed in the USA
LVOW101437041211

257720LV00001B/1/P